Historic Properties
Preservation and the Valuation Process

Historic Properties
Preservation and the Valuation Process

Judith Reynolds, MAI

American Institute of Real Estate Appraisers
430 N. Michigan Ave., Chicago, IL 60611

FOR EDUCATIONAL PURPOSES ONLY

The opinions and statements set forth herein are those of the author and do not necessarily reflect the viewpoint of the American Institute of Real Estate Appraisers or its individual members, and neither the Institute nor its editors and staff assume responsibility for such expressions of opinion or statements.

Foreword

The number of renovation projects and the expanding preservation movement in this country have created a growing need for guidance in valuing historic properties. *Historic Properties: Preservation and the Valuation Process* not only presents methods of appraisal; it attempts to increase awareness of the relationship between real estate and the society it serves. It also provides a detailed look at economic considerations, such as easements, which affect the appraisal of historic properties.

This research volume, which serves as a companion to other Institute monographs, is part of the Institute's continuing effort to develop and maintain the highest standards for the appraisal of all properties.

John D. Dorchester, Jr., MAI
1982 President
American Institute of Real Estate Appraisers

Contents

Introduction

The American public has become interested in the visible evidence of its history that remains in the factories, stores, mansions, and mills of the past. Enthusiasm for reviving these buildings is strengthened by their superior workmanship and materials—rare in much new construction—and by the ongoing reaction to much of modern architecture.

Truly historic, architecturally and culturally significant, and even merely old and interesting properties present a challenge to appraisers; not only do varied social, cultural, and aesthetic aspects impart value, but these are also affected by new interpretations of the meaning of "economic life," which has traditionally been oriented toward new construction. Concepts of the economic life of buildings have had to be greatly expanded as structures are being routinely renovated, restored, and revived, in line with current sensibilities and policies regarding building preservation.

The appraisal of historic or older properties demands an understanding of the relationships between real estate and the society it serves. This includes some knowledge of how both architectural styles and construction techniques are related to history. Some understanding of the preservation movement itself may also be helpful.

Early efforts to preserve and highlight important properties began in the mid-1800s. In 1849 Hasbrouck House in Newburgh, New York, the headquarters of George Washington before the Revolutionary War, was opened as a public museum with the support of the New York state legislature and a group of private citizens. In 1853 in Virginia, the Mount Vernon Ladies Association of the Union began to raise money to save Washington's home on the Potomac, Mount Vernon; by 1859 it was opened to the public. In 1883 Abraham Lincoln's home in Springfield, Illinois became a public museum. In 1893 the Association for the Preservation of Virginia Antiquities acquired 22.5 acres of the old townsite of Jamestown, beginning years of work to conserve and interpret the landing site of the first American colonists. At the turn of the century, similar efforts to preserve early colonial properties in the southwestern part of the United States were also occurring.

The early focus of the preservation movement was on structures associated with well-known figures and events in American history. However, as the movement became widespread in the 1960s and 1970s, it became increasingly centered on architecture. At first, interest had been limited to Colonial structures and to the Neoclassical buildings such as those designed by Thomas Jefferson and Benjamin Latrobe. Eventually the elaborate Victorian structures of the late 19th century became objects of preservationist interest. More recently, the Art Deco style popular in the 1920s and 1930s has been deemed worthy of preservation.

By the late 1970s the preservation movement demonstrated its strength by historic district zoning, widespread adaptive use, and federal tax incentives for preservation.

Another trend increasingly emphasized by the preservation movement is its stabilizing effect on both urban and rural neighborhoods and communities and the protection of the fabric of former ways of life. This trend is concerned with the interaction and ultimate impact of the whole built environment.

Underlying these trends are the economic considerations which are the major concern of real estate appraisers. Preservation was at one time clearly not justifiable in terms of market-supported rates of return. The increased cost of new construction, the special tax benefits and grants provided for preservation, and changed energy consumption standards, however, have rearranged the economics of preservation. At the same time the preferences of the marketplace have also changed.

The following chapters deal with documentation of architectural styles and historical significance, the effect of legislative and regulatory efforts to maintain notable structures, the application of contemporary uses to architecturally appealing but outmoded structures, the mechanism of the preservation easement, and the way in which all these are integrated into the appraisal process itself.

1

Recognizing Historic or Architecturally Significant Properties

Appraising historic property, whether simple data collection or valuation, requires some knowledge of how properties qualify as historic or architecturally significant. The selection of comparable data, the comparison process, the analysis of highest and best use, and the continuous correlation that is carried out during the appraisal process is a weighing of many factors, among which, for the historic property, must be relative historic and architectural significance. Where circumstances warrant, the services of an architectural historian may need to be secured, but appraisers should not be ignorant of this facet of real estate economics.

The concept of historical properties used here embraces (1) historically significant properties, (2) architecturally outstanding structures, (3) adaptive uses of merely old and architecturally interesting properties, and (4) properties that are part of the broad cultural heritage of the country. Technically, historic properties are those associated with persons or events of historical significance, whereas architecturally significant buildings are rare or outstanding examples of architectural styles or periods. The distinction may be blurred for very old and thus very rare structures. Rarity, association with historic events or persons, and architectural excellence may be present alone or in any combination in a property.

The types of properties that may be loosely deemed "historic" range from the United States Capitol to a Midwest Main Street store built by the WPA during the Depression. Furthermore, the associations that impart value vary with time. History is constantly being rewritten and reinterpreted. Events associated with the Civil War, for example, have had a varying emphasis from period to period. The importance of specific historical periods as well as architectural styles is relative and fluctuates, as do all the aspects of real estate that contribute to value.

In 1976, the *AIA Journal* asked 150 architects, historians, and critics to choose the greatest achievements of American architecture of the preceding 200 years. They chose 260 buildings in 140 localities in 36 states, Japan, and Canada.[1] The choices reflect architecture as both art and technology. The panel selected the following seven buildings as top-ranking works of American architecture:

First Place: The University of Virginia
                  Charlottesville, Virginia
                  Thomas Jefferson, 1822–1826

Second Place: Rockefeller Center
                  New York, New York
                  Reinhard & Hoffmeister, Corbett, Harrison, and MacMurray, and Hood & Fouilhoux, 1940

Third Place: Dulles International Airport
(tie)   Chantilly, Virginia
                  Eero Saarinen, 1962

                  Falling Water
                  Bear Run, Pennsylvania
                  Frank Lloyd Wright, 1937

Fourth Place: Carson, Pirie, Scott & Company
                  Chicago, Illinois
                  Louis Sullivan, 1899

Fifth Place: Seagram Building
(tie)   New York, New York
                  Philip Johnson and Mies van der Rohe, 1958

                  Philadelphia Savings Fund Society Building
                  Philadelphia, Pennsylvania
                  George Howe and William Lescaze, 1932

[1] The complete list is presented in the appendix.

A similar poll taken at a different time would undoubtedly produce different choices. For example, the recognition of Thomas Jefferson may have reflected a recent revival of interest in his work.

Although there is no master list ranking all historic and architecturally significant properties, the consensus of informed opinion about the significance of a particular property can usually be ascertained by research that is well within reason for most appraisal assignments.

Documentation

Information on a property's historical or architectural significance is available at the national, state, and local levels from published materials and resource personnel. In addition to the government entities that deal with historic preservation, private and professional organizations can provide documentary information (see Figure l).

National Sources

The National Trust for Historic Preservation, a private nonprofit organization, was chartered by Congress in 1949 to lead the preservation movement. It man-

Figure 1

ages the Endangered Property Fund and the National Preservation Revolving Fund; sponsors seminars and education programs on historic preservation; owns and maintains certain outstanding properties that are open to the public; and accepts and controls preservation easements on other important properties. Through the Preservation Press, the Trust publishes a journal, newsletters, books, and pamphlets. The Trust is also involved in lobbying and in legal and financial aid for historic projects. Income for the National Trust is provided through membership dues, contributions, endowments, and some federal funding. Technical expertise from many sources nationally has been concentrated in this valuable resource.

The National Register of Historic Places, maintained by the Department of the Interior, is the federal government's official list of properties that are significant in American history, architecture, and culture and should be preserved. Although the National Register is an incomplete list of significant properties, it is an important guide for appraisers because of the potential positive or negative effects of listing on property value. The National Register denotes recognition at the highest level and qualifies properties for substantial federal and state tax benefits and grants.

The Economic Recovery Act of 1981 (and the Tax Reform Act of 1976 that preceded it) provide significant benefits to income-producing properties at the national, state, and local levels that have been certified by the Secretary of the Interior. National Register properties automatically qualify; properties in historic districts listed in the National Register must be certified as contributing to the district to qualify. Also eligible are properties in historical districts designated under a state or local statute that have been certified by the Secretary of the Interior as meeting National Register criteria.

The Register, listing more than 25,000 properties, includes individual structures and historic districts, ranging from houses to government buildings and including forts, canals, and archeological sites.

To be listed on the National Register a property must possess:

1. An association with events that have made a significant contribution to history, or
2. An association with the lives of persons significant in our past, or
3. Distinctive characteristics of a type, period, or method of construction, or representation of the work of a master, or possession of special artistic values, or
4. Information important in prehistory or history

Nominations to the National Register are made mainly by individuals through state historic preservation officers; local governments may also make nominations. Owners may now concur or object to the nomination of their property and a majority of owners can prevent the listing of a district.[2] If an owner objects, the property will not be listed but will be kept on a separate list of properties eligible for the Register. Owners may also now petition to remove their property from the Register.

The National Register has grown at a much greater rate since the National Historic Preservation Act of 1966,[3] which expanded the scope of the Register to include sites of local, state, and regional as well as national significance. Before 1966, Register properties were mainly National Historic Landmarks and National Historic Sites.[4] National Historic Landmarks, governed by a detailed set of criteria, are categorized by nine themes ranging from the earliest inhabitants of the country through major American wars and social and humanitarian movements. National Historic Sites are of similar significance but are limited to properties administered by the National Park Service. Properties already listed, and those proposed for inclusion in the Register are listed every February in the *Federal Register*.[5]

National Architectural and Engineering Record: This is an amalgamation of the Historic American Buildings Survey and the Historic American Engineering Record. The documentation of historic buildings has been greatly aided by the Historic American Buildings Survey (HABS), started in 1933 as employment for architects, draftsmen, and photographers. By the end of 1934 more than 3,000 photographs and 5,000 sheets of drawings had been made of public buildings, churches, residences, bridges, forts, barns, mills, rural outbuildings, Indian pueblos, mining settlements, the ruins of early villages along the James River in Virginia, and Russian ruins in Alaska.

The work of HABS has been ongoing although little was done between 1941 and 1957. A typical survey consists of photographs, measured drawings, and narrative description (before World War II, some properties were only photographed). The originals of the drawings and photographs in the Library of Congress are a useful source of information for appraisers interested in a specific

---

[2]P.L. 96-515, 16 USC 470.

[3]P.L. 89-665.

[4]The United States Capitol and its grounds, the Library of Congress, the Supreme Court, and the White House are specifically exempted from the National Register by the National Historic Preservation Law of 1966. They are protected by other provisions of law.

[5]The *Federal Register* is obtainable through the Government Printing Office or through the National Register Office of the Department of the Interior.

property[6] that has been studied. The Historic Sites Act of 1935 assured the continuance of HABS by declaring it a national policy to "preserve for public use historic sites, buildings and objects of national significance for the inspiration and benefit of the people of the United States." Greater support was provided by the 1966 Act. Documentation by HABS is to some extent random. The program in recent years has tended to concentrate on threatened properties and neighborhoods.

In 1958, the American Society of Civil Engineers launched the Historic American Engineering Record (HAER) to cooperate with HABS and the Library of Congress in recording engineering feats. In 1979, HABS and HAER were combined into the National Architectural and Engineering Record (NAER) of the National Park Service. The combined record in the Library of Congress consists of 67,000 photographs, 40,000 measured drawings, and 30,000 pages of description and history covering 20,000 properties.

Local Designation and Historic Districts

Beyond the federal categories of designation and certification are state and local designations that may affect value. Almost every jurisdiction has an historic preservation organization of some type; many municipalities have designated historic districts controlled by local laws. Modification or demolition of properties in these districts is frequently subject to a review process that can significantly affect value.

Research for the Appraiser

Documentation of a property's historical and architectural significance can be researched in the nearest public or historical association library. Local historical societies and state historical commissions are excellent sources of information; many cities have painstakingly rated their buildings as to architectural and historical significance. Each state has a staffed historical preservation office.[7] Property owners are also helpful; many have carried out their own detailed research. Descendants of a famous person with whom a property is associated—whether or not they are involved in ownership—are also potential information sources. The bibliography at the end of this book lists published material that may aid in valuing a specific property.

---

[6]Information concerning reference and photoduplication services is available by writing to the Prints and Photographs Division, Library of Congress, Washington, D.C. 20540.

[7]See Appendix B for list and also for a list of government department and agency liaison offices.

2

Building Styles

Because the quality of architecture can affect market value, and because architecture plays such a central role in measuring historic properties, familiarity with the stylistic patterns of various historical periods is essential. Moreover, many buildings are not pure examples of any one style but are amalgamations of forms in fashion at the time of their construction or renovation.

Following is a brief synopsis of major building styles as they developed in America; more detailed information is available from the architectural history books listed in the bibliography, among others.

The Colonial Period

When the U.S. was settled in the 1600s, there was no indigenous architecture to be adopted by the European colonists. Except for the adobe houses of the Southwest, the structures occupied by the American Indians were not considered suitable. Thus the early phases of building development in the U.S. were characterized by European concepts, styles, and techniques.

Because wood was abundant, most early colonial structures were frame; however, in areas such as Jamestown, Virginia, bricks could be manufactured from the plentiful supply of clay and mortar made from oyster shells so that masonry buildings were built as early as 1611.

Along the eastern seaboard most buildings of the first century of colonization were based on English rural architecture. Houses were simple one- or two-room single-story structures, some with sleeping attics or, less commonly, a second floor. Exposed timber ceilings and large fireplaces were characteristic. In New England chimneys evolved as the central feature of the house, while in Virginia houses had chimneys at the ends.

The colonial buildings of the American Southwest are very different from those of the other colonies. They are in some ways rather primitive, but they are an original, distinctive style, combining Spanish and Indian influence, char-

Colonial, 1610–1720

Early colonial architecture is characterized by simple facades; asymmetrical floor plans, exterior shapes, and elevations (southern buildings are somewhat more symmetrical); hand hewn, heavy timber frames (although brick was common in Virginia); and windows with small panes. The interiors had wood partitions, some plastering, simple panelling, and low ceiling. The exposed framing was frequently bevelled and otherwise embellished. Early windows were casement; double-hung sash was not typical before 1720. The buildings of this period are derived from the medieval vernacular country houses of England. Pictured is a colonial frame dwelling with an atypical extra story; most would be only one and a half stories.

acterized by flat roofs, projecting beams called *vigas,* and hand-finished adobe surfaces.

Seventeenth century churches in the East were generally simple wood or brick structures reflecting their English ancestry; in the Southwest the traditional forms of European church design were executed in the earthy heaviness of mud masonry.

New England's earliest houses were wood-framed and finished with clapboarding. The practice of insulating walls with a mixture of straw and clay or with pieces of brick was later discontinued. The heavy wood framing was held together with mortise and tenon joints. Throughout the period, individual structures—true to the Puritan ideal—remained plain, even austere.

In Virginia architecture evolved to reflect a more comfortable and aristocratic way of life, with the plantation house as the center of political and economic control. Still, seventeenth century builders were mainly artisans, not architects; it was not until the eighteenth century that American architecture took a direction of its own.

10

Mission Style

Mission Style churches were built of stone or adobe. Some were a simple single rectangular enclosure with a nave and a sanctuary; others were cruciform, with a transept between the nave and the sanctuary, often lighted by windows in a dome over the transept. Window openings are small relative to those of churches in other parts of the country. These churches sometimes have vaulted interiors. There are usually one or more towers. Ornamentation varies from primitive to refined. The red tile roofs so prevalent in the Southwest were not manufactured until 1786; earlier roofs were of wood or thatch. The style differs somewhat from state to state.

The Eighteenth Century

In the late seventeenth and the early eighteenth centuries the Mission Style was developed in the Southwest. Most of the buildings surviving are churches. These churches were designed and their construction directed by monks, primarily Franciscans; Indians provided much of the labor. In Mexico the baroque had become a highly developed architectural style, but the mission churches of the Southwest United States were influenced more strongly by the classical as it turned away from the baroque. This trend was foreshadowed by San Estevan at

11

Acoma, New Mexico, built in the early seventeenth century and still relatively intact.

The prevailing architectural style of eighteenth century America was derived from the classical, renaissance, and baroque forms that had dominated Europe since 1650. Repudiating asymmetrical medieval styles, the movement emphasized symmetry, regularity, horizontal form, and classical proportioning. This period is most often called Georgian, after the kings who ruled England between 1714 and 1830.

Evolution Toward the Federal Period

The influence of the English Architect Christopher Wren dominated the design of buildings in both New England and Virginia in the early 1700s. Tall-spired churches and single rectangular block houses with sharply pitched roofs and baroque trim were characteristic. By mid-century baroque aspects had yielded to purer classical Greek and Roman forms, evidenced by the influence of the Italian Renaissance architect Andrea Palladio on the great plantation houses of the South. Palladian design allowed a separateness or wholeness to each component of the unified structure, in sharp contrast to the rectangular block concepts of the earlier part of the century.

As colonial civilization moved westward from the coast, its architecture had become diversified in response to the climate and the availability of building materials. Log cabins, brought to America by the Swedes who settled in Delaware in the 1630s, became the domestic architecture of early settlers in rural areas. The style was easily adaptable to any area where there were large trees to supply the basic building material.

John Marston Fitch, Jr.,[1] has stated that by 1789 four distinctive types of single-family houses in America exemplified the contemporary architecture of the country:

1. The compact New England House, designed for long hard winters and moderate summers, with small windows and small rooms and low ceilings. The prototype was adaptable to wood or brick and to rural or urban use.
2. The Palladian plantation house of the middle seaboard states, designed for hot weather, with high ceilings, large windows, porches, and porticoes.

[1] James Marston Fitch, Jr., *American Building: The Historical Forces That Shaped It* (New York: Schocken Books, 1947, 1948, and 1966), p. 25.

Georgian, 1720–1790

Georgian buildings typically had pitched roofs, a center entrance, and a balanced plan and elevations. Double-hung windows, still with many small panes, were introduced. Early in the period, embellishments were quite complex, in the baroque manner, acquiring a classic balance and simplicity later. Interior structural elements were no longer exposed but were covered with panelling or plaster.

Federal, 1790–1820

In the Federal Period buildings had nearly flat roofs, balustrades, porticoes with columns, and tall narrow windows and chimneys. Side and fan lights were added to entrance doors, which were sometimes recessed. Interiors marked the real departure of the period: Delicate plaster work and oval, circular, and hexagonal spaces were copied from Roman palaces. Fireplace walls were no longer panelled, but plastered; fireplaces were smaller; H and HL hinges gave way to butt hinges. The six-panel door typically had smaller panels at the top. Interior detailing was strongly influenced by the designs of the Adam brothers.

3. The Louisiana French pavilion house with galleries and balconies to shade the house, floor-to-ceiling windows, high ceiling, and central halls.

4. The inward mud masonry hacienda of the Southwest, with thick walls, few windows in the outer facades, and larger windows on the shaded patio.

The Nineteenth Century Federal Period

The much-admired Federal style popular between 1790 and 1820 was a simplification of earlier Georgian architecture and a return to the purity of line and form of ancient Greece and Rome. Ornamentation became generally more restrained; verticality was introduced. This style prevailed on the eastern seaboard with the support of the wealthy mercantile society. Outstanding exponents were

Greek Revival, 1820–1860

The style is identified by pediments and columns, heavy cornices, white-painted exteriors, and strong simple moldings. The focus shifted from the long facades of buildings to the gable ends, which frequently were designed with column-supported entablatures turned toward the street. Chimneys became smaller.

American-born architect Charles Bulfinch of Boston, English-born architect and engineer Benjamin Latrobe, and Scottish architect Robert Adam. Thomas Jefferson's architecture is distinctive; his work, more than that of the others, reflected the ancient Roman ideals that symbolized his political and social beliefs.

Greek Revival

After the War of 1812 Neoclassicism was further refined into the Greek Revival style, which flourished in the U.S. as nowhere else, perhaps because Greece was thought of as the birthplace of democracy and Americans associated the style with their own democratic ideals. Benjamin Latrobe introduced the style with his Bank of Philadelphia in 1798, the first American building to incorporate a classical Greek order, and a model for numerous banks, churches and public buildings, large and small, in every part of the country.

Architect Robert Mills was among those designing monumental Greek Revival buildings in Washington, D.C., to serve the new federal government. His work included the U.S. Treasury Building with its long Ionic colonnade. William Strickland's Second Bank of the United States, built in 1818 in Philadelphia, was based on the design of the Parthenon. Thomas U. Walter's Girard College in Philadelphia, built between 1833 and 1847, consisted of five distinctly spaced Greek temples, the principal one of which has a colonnade on all four sides.

15

Gothic Revival, 1820–1850

The Gothic style is characterized by upward thrusting spires, pointed arches, and ornateness. Medieval symmetry was somewhat offset by a classical balance; the Revival was far from a pure form. A fine example of the style is St. Patrick's Cathedral in New York City, designed by James Renwick. A renewed revival of the style around 1900 produced such anomalies as the Gothic skyscraper.

16

Queen Anne Style, 1875–1895

This is picturesque rather than classical. One of the phases of Queen Anne was the Shingle Style of the 1880s shown here, using shingles to cover the facades as well as the roof. This was more uniform in its form and trim than other turreted and trimmed phases of Queen Anne.

The Industrial Era

As the forces of industrialization and urbanization became dominant in the 19th century, architecture began to change. American mass production spread in the early part of the 19th century from New England to wherever water was available to power the machinery. By the 1830s, steam power was producing standardized sawn and milled lumber. Balloon framing was born in the 1840s after nails began to be mass-produced. The construction of buildings itself became an industry.

During the 19th century innovations introduced into growing urban centers included central water and sewer systems, street paving and cleaning, mass transportation, gas lighting, fuel delivery, and trash and garbage collection. Central heating, refrigeration, and indoor plumbing became prevalent in cities.

At the same time building technology was advancing significantly. Factory buildings required stronger supports than ordinary wood framing; wood trusses and then iron columns were developed. Cast-iron fronts on city buildings were common by the middle of the century. By the end of the century steel framing

17

The Italianate Style, 1850–1870

Italianate architecture has survived in rows of city commercial buildings like the one pictured here. The hallmarks are flat roofs with projecting cornices, arches and columns framing the windows, and the use of cast iron for the facade. The cast iron fronts of the many urban commercial buildings of the era provided both structural support and decorative wide window openings.

was being used in the skyscrapers of the "Chicago Style" of commercial building.

Architecture became a jumble of "picturesque" styles. Gothic Revival was first used for churches and public buildings, then after 1830 for houses. The Italian Villa style derived from the architecture of the Italian countryside became in the 1830s and 1840s a rival of the Gothic. It was characterized by asymmetr-

18

Second Empire Style, 1860–1880

Many massive public buildings were erected in the Second Empire mode, typified by the federal buildings of Arthur B. Mullet in many major American cities; the old State, War, Navy Building in Washington, D.C., is typical. Although inspired by the French architecture of the Second Empire, they were actually more like seventeenth century European buildings than the public buildings being constructed in France in this period. The distinguishing characteristics are the mansard roof, dormer windows, and sculptural detailing.

ical arrangements of square shapes, arched windows, towers, and cupolas. Another expression of the Italian influence was the "Italianate" iron-front commercial row building. Queen Anne, a third picturesque style, emerged in the latter part of the century, mainly as a style for houses; it had the look of the countryside because of its extensive use of wood, informal trim, and extended

19

unboxlike form. Queen Anne is characterized by turrets, varied textures, very large chimneys, oriel windows with many panes, spindle work, terra-cotta ornamentation, porches, shingles, horizontal banding, and the generous use of wood in a naturalistic, expressive manner. Queen Anne began with the "stick style" with its wood diagonal and cross bracing trim and evolved through several phases, culminating in the shingle style. The interiors of Queen Anne houses showed the beginnings of the development of the open plan.

In contrast to the countrified look of Queen Anne and the other picturesque styles, was the refined elegance of the Second Empire style, borrowed from the French, essentially for urban use, exemplified by rows of prestigious townhouses as well as many public buildings. Sometimes called the Mansard style because its chief characteristic is the high, gently sloped roof, Second Empire architecture (corresponding with the reign of Napoleon III from 1852–1870) is strongly vertical. The mansard roof encloses the top floor of the building; there are almost always ornate dormer windows. The windows rest on string courses which mark the floor levels. Stone is the predominant material. Larger buildings have projecting pavilions and sculptured detail.

In the latter part of the nineteenth century for the first time the major concern of construction became the function rather than the beauty of a building. Speculative housing projects—a new concept—appeared. The country was developing almost too fast for architecture to keep pace. In reaction to the Victorian architectural excesses, there were various revivals such as the High Victorian Gothic (1870–1905), Jacobean (1890–1915), Late Gothic (1895–1930), and Georgian Revival (1885–1940).

Romanesque

Out of the chaotic mid-nineteenth century, with its hiatus in construction during the Civil War, came an architect of the first rank, Henry Hobson Richardson. He developed to excellence the Romanesque Revival style, many fine examples of which remain. With its rounded arches, heavy stone texture and short, strong columns, Romanesque achieves a ruggedness and a massiveness, frequently dark-hued, but with order and vigor provided by arches and by clarity of organization.

Richardson Romanesque bridges the classicism of the Greek Revival style and the originality and exuberance of the Chicago style that developed after the Chicago fire of 1871. Among those influenced by Richardson's ordered romanticism was Louis Sullivan, who designed the Chicago Auditorium after he had seen one of Richardson's designs.

Romanesque Revival, 1845–1910

This architecture is based on load-bearing masonry construction, typically with round arches, including those used to frame large door openings. The overall effect of massiveness yet simplicity and clarity was achieved using a heavy and rough stone texture, a single tower as a focal point, and short, strong columns. This architecture was popular for churches, railroad stations, schools, libraries and federal buildings. Marshall Field's wholesale store building in Chicago in 1885 was in this style. The early commercial buildings of Seattle and other north-western cities were strongly influenced by the Romanesque style.

Chicago Style

The Chicago School office buildings were an original American form of architecture, one that combined powerfully expressed modern technology with late nineteenth century ornamentation. Sullivan was an outstanding architect who had a command of complex structural design as well as versatility. During this era, multi-story office buildings evolved, as exemplified by Chicago's 16-story Monadnock Building (completed in 1891 and currently being restored) and the steel-framed skyscrapers of the modern era, although the first elevator office building in the U.S. was the Equitable Life Assurance Building completed in 1870 in New York City. In contrast to the office buildings of the Chicago school, the Equitable building was in the Second Empire style, complete with mansard rood, entablatures, and classical columns.

In 1899, Louis Sullivan built one of his masterpieces, the Carson, Pirie, Scott & Co. department store in Chicago, but the Chicago school era was almost over.

The 1893 Columbian Exposition held in Chicago was directed by city planner and architect Daniel Burnham, who turned his back on the Chicago Style and promoted a return of Neoclassicism, this time on a grand imperial scale. The impressive buildings set on Chicago's lakefront succeeded in shifting architectural thinking throughout the country back to Greek and Roman styles. Under this influence, the master plan for Washington, D.C., originally prepared by Pierre Charles L'Enfant in the early nineteenth century, was revived by the McMillan Commission in 1902. Washington's Union Station, on a grand Roman scale, soon followed. The Federal Triangle national government office buildings continued the revival of Neoclassic styles through the 1930s in Washington and in other cities.

Beaux Arts

L'Ecole des Beaux Arts was a French school providing classical training in architecture and other arts. The academic principles taught there were incorporated into the classical Renaissance revival that occurred as a result of the Columbian Exposition. These principles include the massing of large-scale, classical elements in a formalized functional manner. The first major example of Beaux Arts Style in the U.S. was the Boston Public Library designed by Charles McKim, of McKim, Mead, & White, in 1888.

New York City's Pennsylvania Station, built between 1906 and 1910, was an outstanding example of the many railroad stations built according to Beaux Arts principles. Columns are often used in pairs to indicate their load-bearing function. Many buildings have large flights of stairs and classical sculptures.

Chicago Style, 1880–1893

Elevator office buildings, in which walls and floors were for the first time supported by the steel building frames, were the main focus of the Chicago "style" or "school" of architecture. Most buildings were clad in gray or brown terra-cotta and were ornamented. The bands of windows were indented and there were elaborate projecting cornices.

Beaux Arts, 1895–1910

The Beaux Arts style was used to create stately urban dwellings like the one shown here, but its more recognized expression is in massive public buildings and train stations with their grandness of scale, columns, flights of marble stairs, and squareness.

The central portion of the building dominates the structure; other portions of the building are demonstrated by their smaller size to be of lesser importance. Interior spaces were usually intricate but highly ordered.

The Twentieth Century

The early twentieth century was another period of eclecticism and confusion. Coming to the architectural forefront during this time was Frank Lloyd Wright, whose "Prairie Style" houses and solid, vertically-oriented office buildings were highly innovative both architecturally and technologically.

The contributions to modern American architecture of Richardson, Sullivan, and Wright, each succeeding the other directly, and with the line of influence following the succession, were outstanding. All three were based in Chicago, but the effect of their work extended to the boundaries of the country and beyond.

24

Art Nouveau, 1880–1920

Art Nouveau replaced Greek or Roman elements such as columns and pediments with curved, zigzag, or geometric shapes and fanciful ornamentation. Art Deco, the decorative style that followed, is sometimes fairly simplistic with lineal ornamentation, but, as can be seen, some of the decorative elements may be fairly intricate. Art Deco encompasses geometrical shapes and curvilinear forms.

During the uncertainties of the early twentieth century Wright's work emerged as unique and cohesive. His houses had a minimal number of rooms, with spaces flowing into one another. Ornamental excesses were repudiated and buildings were integrated with their sites. Wright used concrete as no one had before, in blocks and great slabs reinforced with steel rods, and in continuous curvilinear forms. He eliminated basements and trimmed away other features he considered extraneous. He designed furniture and fixtures as integral components of his buildings.

25

Art Nouveau

Art Nouveau, also called Art Moderne, developed in Europe in the late nineteenth century. It began as a fanciful style that consciously avoided the traditional. Art Deco, the decorative style of the 1930s, followed Art Nouveau; both include elements of technology, symbolism, functionalism, and naturalism. The overall movement began with a curvilinear style decorated with vegetational shapes. About 1910 it became more rectilinear and the naturalistic, foliate, aspects were surrendered. After 1918 it mostly emphasized cubic geometry. Art Nouveau and Art Deco were the architecture of transition from the elaborate architecture of the 1890s to the severe geometry of the International style which emerged after World War I.

International Style

In 1932 an exhibit of contemporary European architecture at the Museum of Modern Art in New York launched the International Style, inspired by the German Bauhaus school of design. Although Bauhaus design was originally directed at housing for workers (stemming as it did from the socialism that spread through Germany after World War I), in the U.S. it was expressed in every possible kind of structure.

Technological advances and simplification are characteristic of the International Style, which was dominated by the work of Walter Gropius, Marcel Breuer, Charles Eduoard LeCorbusier, Mies van der Rohe, Philip Johnson, and Louis Kahn.

City planning also came to the fore. In 1858 Frederick Law Olmstead's design for New York City's Central Park engendered an effort across the country to beautify cities, but very little organized city planning was carried out before Radburn, New Jersey, the first planned community, was begun in 1929.

Rockefeller Center became the first "urban renewal" project. Begun in 1928 and under construction through 1940, it was strongly influenced by Beaux Arts principles as well as European modernism. The center's office towers were built as shafts—detached slabs, with shallow bays and many windows around a central utility core.

The design of office towers in New York and many other cities has been influenced by zoning requirements that exchange the bonus of greater height and density for setbacks. The face of urban America was irrevocably altered in the modern era from the row buildings of the nineteenth century.

New office buildings of the late 1970s and early 1980s have displayed a turning away from the severity of the International style. Buildings have a sculptured, rather than a streamlined appearance, and hard lines have been softened.

International, 1930–1970

Exemplified by skyscraper construction, this style dropped the cornices, ornamentation and terra-cotta exteriors of earlier Chicago school buildings and emphasized a streamlined appearance. The curtain wall evolved and windows were set flush to further the streamlined effect.

The texture and substance of exterior walls have once again become important, while the metal skeleton of the building and its minimalist metal and glass sheathing have retreated. There has been somewhat of a return to the ordered geometry of the Beaux Arts style.

Ongoing changes in architecture affect the relative market appeal of all buildings; the architectural preferences of buyers and tenants affect value. If the market demonstrates an increment or a detriment attributable to historicity or architecture, appraisers need to modify their judgments accordingly.

3

Public Policy and the Process of Appraisal

Public policy toward historic properties obviously has impact on their value. Appraisers need to be aware of the positive and negative attitudes that owners bring to the marketplace in response to historic designations.

On one side, historic designation can provide tax benefits and rehabilitation subsidies; on the other, it brings to the fore the conflict between preservation as a regulated policy and the traditional rights of property owners to use, modify, or replace existing structures. Today government policy adds another major facet to the determination of highest and best use. Historic district zoning and landmark preservation laws take the concept of zoning, as it has heretofore been known in this country, a significant step further. Zoning as a right of government has long been accepted by property owners and users, but zoning must constantly be revised as economic conditions change. The need for such flexibility and the concept of historic district zoning are basically in conflict; the impasse is bound to be detrimental to many properties at one time or another.

Federal Policy

The Historic Sites act of 1935 declared that "it is a national policy to preserve for public use historic sites, buildings, and objects of national significance for the inspiration and benefit of the people of the United States." Although the statement is unequivocal, the program is somewhat vague in its scope and objectives. The U.S. has no single federal department charged solely with building preservation (as does France, for instance, where the Service dés Monuments Historiques, founded in 1831, functions as a strong national ministry); the Department of the Interior has the most significant role in conservation and preservation.[1]

Earlier national preservation efforts were grounded in the Antiquities Act of 1906, which protected historic resources on federally owned land; the National Park Service Organic Act of 1916, which established the Service to administer parks, including the historic features therein; and the Historic Sites Act of 1935, which created the Historic Landmarks Program.

The 1966 Historic Preservation Act provided the main thrust for involvement by the federal government in historic preservation by (1) requiring the Secretary of the Interior to expand and maintain the National Register of Historic Places as the official inventory of the cultural property of national, state and local significance; (2) establishing the Advisory Council on Historic Preservation to protect registered properties from adverse effects of federally supported programs; and (3) providing for matching grants-in-aid to states and to the National Trust for Historic Preservation. Both the Advisory Council and the grants-in-aid programs have been substantially weakened by the economic cutbacks of the early 1980s.

The National Register and Public Policy

The National Register of Historic Places functions as a major instrument of public preservation policy. Listing on the National Register is the single most important criterion triggering legislated benefits or penalties to owners of historic properties. Approximately 10 percent of the 25,000 listed properties are historic districts and each of these districts contains hundreds or even thousands of individual properties. The impact of the expansion of the National Register since 1966 has been very significant in terms of the number of properties affected.

Most nomination forms for the National Register are completed by State Historic Preservation Officers, whose staffs include experts in history, architecture, and archaeology. Nomination forms are reviewed by a state review board, signed by the State Historic Preservation Officer, and forwarded to the Keeper of the National Register. Each state is required by the 1966 act to publish an inventory and analysis of the state's historic resources. Many states have a state register, some of which may duplicate the National Register.

The Advisory Council on Historic Preservation, created by the 1966 act, is

[1]The certification of properties and their rehabilitation for eligibility for the benefits of the Economic Recovery Tax Act of 1981 (and for the 1976 Tax Reform Act before it) is one of the major responsibilities of the Department of the Interior; see Chapter 4 for a full discussion.

responsible for protecting National Register properties and those eligible for nomination that are threatened by federal projects. The Council is an independent agency of the Executive Branch, made up of cabinet members, government agency administrators, the chairman of the National Trust, a governor, and experts in preservation appointed by the President.

Other Federal Legislation

The Archaeological and Historic Preservation Act of 1974 protects historic and archeaological materials and data from loss as a result of federal construction or federally licensed or aided activities.

The Public Buildings Cooperative Use Act of 1976 directs the Administrator of the General Services Administration (GSA) to give priority to the acquisition or leasing of historic or architecturally significant buildings by government agencies when feasible. The chairman of the Advisory Council on Historic Preservation is responsible for identifying eligible buildings; eligibility is not limited to National Register properties.

The Economic Recovery Tax Act of 1981 (ERTA) establishes tax incentives for the preservation and rehabilitation of historic properties (see Chapter 4). ERTA was preceded by the Tax Reform Act of 1976 and the Revenue Act of 1978, which provided the first accelerated depreciation schedules and investment tax credits for older properties.

Federal Programs

A Department of the Interior grant-in-aid program at one time reimbursed owners of individually registered properties or those in historic districts for up to 50 percent of rehabilitation costs, including acquisitions, surveys, and plans. A grantee had to attach a covenant to the deed agreeing to preserve the property for a number of years—from five years for a grant under $20,000 to 20 years for a grant of more than $100,000. The rehabilitation work had to be visible from a public street or road or the property had to be open to the public for a limited period each year. Though this program has become inactive, the appraiser may be confronted with properties encumbered by the covenants.

The Department of the Interior since the beginning of 1981 has been limiting its responsibilities to federally owned properties and relinquishing responsibility for other historic properties to the states and the National Trust. The annual appropriations to the National Trust are likely to be replaced by a one-time endowment. This will undoubtedly require the National Trust to limit its programs.

The Department of Housing and Urban Development's Urban Development

Action Grant (UDAG) program is aimed at revitalizing central city income properties. The UDAG program emphasizes local, private initiative and a rapid federal response; it has become important to the growing national movement to protect cities and established communities. Essentially UDAGs are second mortgages, closing the gap between first mortgages and the amounts of financing required. UDAGs can help or hinder preservation efforts; for instance, if a UDAG is granted to build a new downtown shopping mall, Main Street may be benefitted but the new mall may replace or be incompatible with existing historic structures. There have been numerous conflicts between the UDAG program and preservation groups, including the Advisory Council on Historic Preservation.

Both HUD and the Department of the Interior provide for community development block grants. In early 1982 the federal Office of Management and Budget proposed phasing out the UDAG and the community development block grants.

As yet there has been no comprehensive determination of which structures are worthy of preservation and how they are to be chosen, although the National Register is becoming the means for achieving that goal. For the appraiser, it is essential to realize the ways in which various levels of government, with their enormous resources, can substantially affect real estate values.

Court Decisions

Recent court decisions have established a strong legal foundation for landmark protection laws which formerly were thought to infringe on property rights guaranteed by the Constitution. Appraisers must thus treat historic designations as they do zoning regulations—that is, as property controls that the government may create and uphold.

The Supreme Court dramatically influenced preservation policy in the U.S. with its 1977 decision in the Grand Central Terminal case.[2] The decision, in essence, affirmed the constitutionality of New York City's landmark preservation ordinance. The question was whether the Penn Central Railroad could construct an office tower over the existing terminal, which had been built in 1913. In 1967 New York City had designated the terminal a landmark under its local ordinance. Two years later, because operation of the terminal alone was no longer economic, Penn Central applied for a permit to build an office tower

---

[2]Penn Central Transportation Company vs. City of New York, 438 U.S. 104, 98 S. Ct. 2646.

above the terminal. The city's Landmark Commission turned down the application. An alternate plan was developed but that plan was also disapproved.

At issue in the case were many elements, chief among them preservation, the law, and economics. The preservationists believed that the office tower would be incongruous with the station; the owners believed they had the right to remedy their uneconomic position. The railroad sued the City of New York on the grounds that there had been a "taking" without compensation. After nine years of litigation that sharply divided New York courts, the U.S. Supreme Court found that no taking had occurred. Cited were the fact that New York law allows property owners a "reasonable" return from landmark properties, permits them to transfer development rights to nearby sites, and offers tax relief if a landmark ceases to be economically viable. The Court also stated that society had helped create the value of the terminal and society had the right to benefit from its preservation.

Grand Central Station was thus preserved and the Penn Central Railroad was denied the right to construct a multi-story office building over it, even though the terminal was designed to carry the additional load, and the zoning would have permitted it.

The decision immediately encouraged other jurisdictions to enact more stringent laws protecting historic properties. One of the most stringent is the Historic Landmark and Historic District Protection Act of the District of Columbia, drafted during the Penn Central litigation, passed soon after the Supreme Court decision, and effective early in 1979. Under this law not only is demolition or alteration of any landmark building or any building in a landmark district prohibited, but an *application* for designation to landmark status can stop a developer's plans even at an advanced stage. Exceptions to the prohibition on demolition or alteration are costly and time-consuming to secure, and the risk of failure is great.

By stating that landmark laws are constitutional, the Supreme Court has in effect changed the highest and best use—defined as the most profitable, legally permitted use—for those properties with landmark designations.

The designation of a property as a national, state, or local landmark does not prevent its demolition unless the laws of the jurisdiction so provide. However, if court injunctions to delay demolition can be obtained on the basis that the property qualifies as a landmark, demolition, although not legally forbidden, can become so expensive as to be prohibitive. Reinterpretation of old laws in a more restrictive fashion is changing the economic expectations of many property owners.

Appraisals must reflect these altered economic expectations. Risk and uncertainty for income-earning properties may be significantly increased; on the other hand, short-term tax benefits may accrue to designated properties. Each property must be considered on an individual basis as it is affected by beneficial and detrimental factors.

State and Local Programs and Legislation

Most states have passed legislation affecting historic properties. However, state and local programs generally lag well behind the federal, and local governments may even be antagonistic to preservation programs tied to federal funding. State-created opportunities for local preservation programs are sometimes ignored.

Since 1966, state historic preservation offices have been established in all states. These offices administer any available federal matching funds, which can be used by private organizations and individuals. Some states have privately administered revolving funds to take threatened properties off the market by direct or option purchase. These properties can then be sold to investors with a covenant to preserve them; the acquisition money goes back into the revolving fund. Such properties are kept on the tax rolls and do not become a continuing drain on preservation funds.

The Historic Preservation Act of 1966 is largely regulatory; it has created a preservation bureaucracy at the state as well as the national level. Applications to the National Register are processed at the state level and there is generally a significant ongoing process of investigation and preparation of case studies. Guidance in preservation matters is available to local jurisdictions from the state offices.

The authority to create and regulate local historic districts usually comes from state-enabling legislation granting municipalities or counties the authority to establish historic districts under their general zoning powers.

After a local historic district is established, typically the local governing body—the city council or commission—is authorized to appoint a board or commission to review proposed construction, demolition, or architectural changes within the historic district before appropriate permits can be issued. Public hearings or comments are sometimes sought. The scope of review varies among local jurisdictions. Some can control all structural changes and all new construction; some are concerned only with exterior changes to buildings built before a certain date. Local governments can typically designate individual properties as local landmarks and regulate them similarly. It is important for appraisers to be familiar with local landmark laws and the effects on locally designated properties.

34

The neighborhood historic district concept, which embodies the idea of preservation of the community-wide built environment, is to some extent replacing that of the preservation of history. The sociological turn that the preservation movement has taken began with the fact that the local restoration society, whether private or public, often became the only neighborhood organization speaking for the community, especially where community organization was at a low point as a result of the exodus from cities to the suburbs.

Decentralization of preservation programs is now a counter-trend, succeeding the intensification of the federal focus on preservation resulting from the 1966 Act. Local ordinances that are inordinately harsh may be modified in the future as economic pressures mount. The property rights that have been surrendered through historic district zoning may or may not be restored. The appraiser should be aware of all of these public policy possibilities as they evolve.

4

The Effect of Tax Provisions

Tax laws since the late 1960s have encouraged building preservation and rehabilitation, principally residential structures. The Tax Reform Act of 1969 allowed a five-year (60-month) write-off of rehabilitation costs for low- and mod-
erate-income housing. Community block grants and low-interest rate
rehabilitation loans provided further incentives to residential reinvestment. The
revitalization of urban neighborhoods was encouraged by the 1974 Housing Act
and by the Housing and Community Development Act of 1977, which included
the Community Reinvestment Act. The donation of a preservation easement to
a properly qualifying charitable organization has been eligible for an income tax
deduction since 1964;[1] the bulk of the properties on which easements were donated before 1976 were residential properties. By 1975, rehabilitation of older
housing stock was a well-established trend, resulting from energy shortages, a
reaction to suburban homogeneity, labor costs, scarcity of building materials,
and inflation.

Although the economic, social, and aesthetic satisfactions of rehabilitation
of older houses were well-established by the mid-1970s, commercial buildings
were still largely neglected. The rehabilitation of commercial structures is economically more complex; it tends to attract community resistance and local governmental interference to a much greater degree than does residential rehabilitation.

The Tax Reform Act of 1976 and the Revenue Act of 1978 provided substantial benefits, especially rapid amortization and investment tax credits, for
the rehabilitation of older income-producing structures. There were also penalties for demolition of historic buildings. The 1976 Act offered a choice: a five-
year write-off of rehabilitation costs or an accelerated depreciation schedule.
Depreciating demolition costs and expenses were prohibited, as was accelerated
depreciation for replacement buildings: previously the cost of, and losses asso-

---

[1]Through various Revenue and Letter Advice Rulings.

ciated with, demolition could be added to the depreciable base of the replacement building.

The 1978 Act permitted a 10 percent investment credit for the rehabiltation of properties that had been used to produce income for at least twenty years. A taxpayer could not take both the 10 percent investment credit and the five-year amortization, but could combine the accelerated depreciation of a rehabilitated property's entire basis with the 10 percent investment credit. To qualify for five-year amortization or accelerated depreciation, a structure and its rehabilitation had to be "certified" by the Department of the Interior (at first by the Heritage Conservation and Recreation Service, later by the National Park Service). These tax benefits often constituted the crucial financial difference that made rehabilitation projects possible.

The 1976 Act had provided for charitable contribution deductions for preservation easements, but with an expiration date of June 14, 1981. The Tax Treatment Extension Act of 1980 makes the deduction for preservation easements permanent. To be eligible, properties must be certified by the Department of the Interior as contributing to the historic district in which they are located. Certification is automatic if the property is listed on the National Register.

The Economic Recovery Tax Act of 1981

The Economic Recovery Tax Act of 1981 (ERTA) substituted a new set of incentives for the preservation and rehabilitation of older structures. These will intensify the impact on real estate of the previous tax legislation.

ERTA is very favorable to preservation. Besides replacing the traditional system of depreciating real property over its economic life with an accelerated cost recovery system (ACRS) period of fifteen years, it provides for substantial tax credits for renovations of older property begun after January 1, 1982. The most favorable of these is a 25 percent tax credit for certified historic structures, whether commercial, industrial, or residential rental properties. For commercial and industrial buildings 30 years or older, there is a 15 percent investment tax credit and for buildings 40 years or older, a 20 percent investment tax credit. Each of the investment tax credits can be combined with the fifteen-year ACRS but the tax credit must be deducted from the depreciable basis unless the property is certified as historic. For certified historic properties renovated according to the Secretary of the Interior's guidelines, the entire shell and rehabilitation cost can be written off using the straight-line method over fifteen years, thus allowing depreciation of 100 percent of rehabilitation expenditures.[2]

---

[2]Late in 1982 this provision was modified. As a result, one-half of the 25 percent rehabilitation tax credit now must be deducted from the property's depreciable basis.

The proportion of tax credit subject to recapture decreases 20 percent with each year the property is held, so that at the end of five years there is no recapture penalty, for either historic or nonhistoric properties. ERTA retained the provision of the TRA of 1976 denying federal income tax deductions for historic building demolition costs or losses. The provision is not particularly significant in preventing demolition if new owners are willing to capitalize demolition costs and the remaining bases of demolished structures.

These provisions may affect the market value of older and historic properties. The government subsidy through tax credits allows investors to accept lower initial equity returns and therefore provides justification for lower overall capitalization rates. The competition to acquire eligible properties is likely to drive up prices.

The Certification Process

To qualify for the 25 percent investment tax credit of ERTA, and for the preservation easement charitable deduction, a property must be federally certified as historic. Older properties that are eligible for certification have a potential for value enhancement that the others lack. The certification process was not altered by the 1981 legislation.

To qualify for certification, a property must be (1) listed on the National Register of Historic Places (these properties are automatically certified), (2) in a district listed on the Register and certified as contributory to the district, or (3) certified as contributory to a district created by a state or local statute that itself is certified by the Department of the Interior as consistent with the standards developed for the National Register listings. A locally-designated property not in a historic district and not eligible for the National Register does not qualify. Buildings less than 50 years old generally do not qualify as contributory to a historic district but otherwise the standards are interpreted liberally, with all buildings that are consistent with the general character of a district qualifying.

Rehabilitation must be separately certified as consistent with the historic character of the structure, and must preserve 75 percent of the existing walls. Rehabilitation includes any work within the original walls and foundation, including modern plumbing and electrical wiring required by building codes. Even construction of a small addition to house a second stairway or an elevator can qualify if installation within the original walls would be detrimental to the integrity of the building. Other additions and landscaping are classified as new construction and are not eligible for tax credit.

Certification forms, available from State Historic Preservation Offices, or the Department of the Interior, require information on ownership, location, architectural detail and distinctions, dates of construction, photographs, and maps. Part I requires a description of the structure, its significant features, and its contribution to the historic district. Part II is used to describe the rehabilitation work and its effect on the exterior and interior of the building. (See pages 41 and 42 for a sample of the form.) The forms are reviewed by the State Historic Preservation Officer (SHPO) and forwarded to the Department of the Interior. If the SHPO fails to process the form in 45 days, it may be submitted directly to the Department of the Interior. The information is reviewed against the Secretary of the Interior's *Standards for Evaluating Structures within Historic Districts,* which are based on National Register criteria. Rehabilitation work is measured by broad standards[3] designed to prevent damage to the historical and architectural integrity of rehabilitated buildings. Generally they preclude sandblasting, the addition of inconsistent architectural elements, and the alteration of the basic character of the buildings.

Certification can, though it usually does not, take as long as six months. However, developers report that the process is usually surprisingly painless. Owners of structures within local or state designated districts not on the National Register, however, must first have the statute certified, then the district certified, and finally the structure certified. Only an authorized representative of the governmental body that enacted the state or local statute may request its certification.

On behalf of the Secretary of the Treasury, the IRS develops and administers all regulations on historic preservation tax incentives. The regulations explain who may claim tax deductions and which historic structures qualify as depreciable and distinguish between new construction and rehabilitation expenses.

Ad Valorem and Other Benefits

Some local jurisdictions offer incentives for the preservation of historic properties through a reduction in annual property taxes. This type of relief is not widespread; nor is it widely endorsed by the public, perhaps because it seems to subsidize a particular class of property owners. Furthermore, since property taxes are the chief revenue source for most local jurisdictions, any decrease in the tax base may be viewed as counter-productive to the general welfare.

Without the necessary state enabling laws, local governments lack the au-

---

[3]The printed standards are available from the Technical Preservation Service, National Park Service, Washington, D.C. 20240.

HISTORIC PRESERVATION CERTIFICATION APPLICATION
Instructions

(Pursuant to Section 2124 of the Tax Reform Act of 1976)

Read the following instructions carefully before filling out the attached application.

The Historic Preservation Certification Application must be completed by taxpayers requesting historic preservation certifications pursuant to the Tax Reform Act of 1976 (P.L. 94-455 90 Stat 1519) made by the Secretary of the Interior. The application is to be filled out in accord with regulations set forth in Chapter I, Title 36 of the Code of Federal Regulations, Part 67 and the instructions given below.

Parts 1 and 2 of this application may be completed and sent to the appropriate State Historic Preservation Officer at any time during the year and may be sent separately or as a single package. A current list of State Historic Preservation Officers may be obtained by writing to:

Tax Reform Act
Office of Archeology and
Historic Preservation
Department of the Interior
Washington, D.C. 20240.

Use typewriter or print clearly in dark ink to complete the application form. If additional space is needed to complete Part 1, use a plain sheet of paper clearly indicating the owner's name and mailing address. If additional space is needed to complete Part 2, use one or more continuation sheets.

COMPLETING PART 1.

Part 1 of the Historic Preservation Certification Application must be completed by owners of structures within Registered Historic Districts requiring a determination from the Secretary of the Interior on whether or not their structure is of historic significance to the district. Depreciable structures individually listed in the National Register are "certified historic structures" for purposes of the Tax Reform Act; owners of these structures need not complete Part 1 (verification of National Register listing may be obtained from the appropriate State Historic Preservation Officer).

IF COMPLETING PART 1:

1. Provide correct name, address, including street, county, city, state and zip code for the structure under consideration. Provide the name of the historic district as listed in the National Register of Historic Places.

2. Briefly describe the general exterior appearance of the structure: include appropriate landscape features and outbuildings; number of stories; type of construction; alterations (with approximate dates). Also describe distinctive interior architectural features or spaces: include hardware, stairways, woodwork, fireplaces.

3. Provide a brief statement describing the significance of the structure. If historically significant, list important persons or events associated with the structure. If architec-turally significant, indicate architect and builder, if known, and describe architectural significance. Give dates of construction and alterations, if known, and check whether on original site or moved.

4. Provide name, mailing address, and telephone number of owner. All Part 1 applications must be signed and dated by the property owner, and returned to the appropriate State Historic Preservation Officer.

Photographs—Recent photographs showing the present appearance of the structure prior to rehabilitation must accompany this application. Photographs are not returnable and should

—show all street elevations and distinctive interior and exterior architectural details.

—be labeled to include property name and brief description of what is shown.

—be black and white or color and be large enough to show architectural details clearly.

—be attached in the upper right corner of the application form with a staple or paperclip.

Maps—A map clearly locating the structure within the boundaries of the Registered Historic District must accompany the application.

All requests for certification of significance are evaluated for conformance with the Secretary of the Interior's "Standards for Evaluating Structures within Historic Districts." These standards, set forth in Department of the Interior procedures 36 CFR Part 67.5, are available by writing to: Tax Reform Act, Office of Archeology and Historic Preservation, Department of the Interior. Washington, D.C. 20240.

Notification as to certification of significance will be made by the Secretary of the Interior in accord with regulations set forth in 36 CFR Part 67.

COMPLETING PART 2.

Part 2 of the Historic Preservation Certification Application must be completed by all owners of certified historic structures wanting their rehabilitation certified by the Secretary of the Interior as being consistent with the historic character of the structure or the district in which the structure is located, thus qualifying as "certified rehabilitation." Part 2 may be used to describe either proposed or completed rehabilitation work.

Wherever possible, Part 2 should be completed prior to the initiation of rehabilitation work. Taxpayers will be notified in writing whether or not the proposed project is consistent with the Secretary of the Interior's "Standards for Rehabilitation" set forth in 36 CFR Part 67.7. Copies of the Standards and guidelines for applying the Standards are available by writing to. Tax Reform Act, Office of Archeology and Historic Preservation.

FHR-8-253 (10-78)

Form Approved
OMB No. 42-R1765

UNITED STATES DEPARTMENT OF THE INTERIOR
Washington D.C. 20243

HISTORIC PRESERVATION CERTIFICATION
APPLICATION — PART 1
(Pursuant to the Tax Reform Act of 1976)

Instructions: *Applicant should read the instructions carefully before completing application. No Certification may be made unless a completed application form has been received (P L. 94-455) Use typewriter or print clearly in dark ink to complete the application form. If additional space is needed to complete Part 1, use the reverse side or a separate plain sheet of paper clearly indicating the owner's name and mailing address. Part 1 of this application may be completed and sent to the appropriate State Historic Preservation Officer at any time during the year, and may be sent separately or with Part 2.*

PART 1 EVALUATION OF SIGNIFICANCE

1. **NAME OF PROPERTY:** _____

Address of property Street _____

City _____ County _____ State _____ Zip Code _____

Name of historic district in which property is located _____

2. **DESCRIPTION OF PHYSICAL APPEARANCE:**
(see instructions for map and photograph requirements—use reverse side if necessary)

3. **STATEMENT OF SIGNIFICANCE:**
(use reverse side if necessary)

Date of construction (if known) _____ ☐ Original site ☐ Moved Date of alterations (if known) _____

4. **NAME AND MAILING ADDRESS OF OWNER:**

Name _____

Street _____

City _____ State _____ Zip Code _____

Telephone Number (during day) Area Code _____

I hereby attest that the information I have provided is. to the best of my knowledge. correct. and that I am owner of the property described above

Signature _____ Date _____

For office use only

The structure described above is included within the boundaries of the National Register historic district and ☐ contributes ☐ does not contribute to the character of the district

The structure ☐ appears ☐ does not appear to meet National Register Criteria for Evaluation (36 CFR 60.6) and ☐ will likely ☐ will not be nominated to the National Register in accord with the Department of the Interior procedures (36 CFR 60)

The structure is located in a district which ☐ appears ☐ does not appear to meet National Register Criteria for Evaluation (36 CFR 60 6). ☐ will likely ☐ will not be nominated to the National Register in accord with Department of the Interior procedures (36 CFR 60). and ☐ appears ☐ does not appear to contribute to the character of said district

Signature _____ Date _____
         State Historic Preservation Officer

This property has been evaluated according to the criteria and procedures set forth by the Department of the Interior (36 CFR 67) and, if subject to depreciation under section 167 of the Internal Revenue Code of 1954.
☐ is hereby certified a historic structure.
☐ does not contribute to the character of the historic district and does not merit certification as a historic structure. Reasons given on the attached sheet

Signature _____ Date. _____
         Keeper of the National Register

42

thority to grant property tax relief. Yet in some states legislation allowing localities to grant tax relief as an incentive to preservation has never been used by any city or county government.

Where ad valorem incentives have been used, they take several forms. One is a moratorium on property tax increases for a period of from five to twenty years, depending on the state. This is generally offered to owners who substantially rehabilitate or restore a significant property.

Another incentive is that the property will be assessed on the basis of a use consistent with its historical integrity if that use is maintained for a given period. This becomes a benefit if the most economic use of the property would produce a much higher assessment, such as would accrue to a commercially-zoned property improved with a mansion in single-family use which could be demolished to develop an office building. There are generally provisions to recover the differential in taxes if the covenants are broken.

A North Carolina law authorizes deferral of 50 percent of annual taxes for properties meeting National Register criteria. Another form of this type of incentive accrues to properties owned by tax-exempt organizations.

A moratorium on increases in taxes can be a powerful incentive to preserve a building that would otherwise be of questionable profitability in the first years after rehabilitation. This type of program has worked well in New York City to encourage widespread renovation of formerly dilapidated though not necessarily "historic" buildings, particularly the loft buildings of Soho.

Although the donation of a partial interest in a property in the form of a conservation or preservation easement is well established as a deduction from income taxes, only a few jurisdictions direct local assessors to consider open space and preservation easements when valuing properties—even though to qualify, an easement must be donated in perpetuity and its restrictions must be permanent restrictions on the use and development of the property.[4]

---

[4]This type of easement is discussed in detail in Chapter 9.

5
Adaptive Uses

"Adaptive use means simply that buildings are modified to some degree to meet contemporary demand."[1] Renewing exisiting structures for new uses and new forms of old uses has become part of both commercial and residential construction; the scope of this activity is in billions of dollars. It provides broadened opportunities for developers, construction companies, architects, engineers, artisans, lawyers, accountants, and, consequently, appraisers.

Appraisal theory and methodology have been traditionally oriented to new construction; appraisal problems, for the most part, have been focused on new buildings, new sites, and the reuse of land—not buildings. This will probably continue, but not to the same extent. Supplies of land, energy, and raw materials are subject to significant limitations. The reuse of existing structures to conserve land, energy, and raw materials appears necessary for economic survival, at least until technology brings about a new industrial revolution. If at the same time architectural history is preserved and the cultural environment enriched, adaptive use can result in enormous social benefits.

Adaptive Use and Economic Trends

Buildings with historic or architectural merit are saved for one of three reasons: (1) a government agency or private charitable organization is willing to carry out the preservation effort because it is consistent with an avowed policy; (2) preserving the property is an emotional issue; or (3) preserving the property is economic. Subsidized and emotionally-directed efforts are now generally confined to historic or architecturally significant properties that are anomalous to

[1]Tony P. Wrenn and Elizabeth D. Mulloy, *America's Forgotten Architecture* (New York: Pantheon Books, 1976), p. 271.

45

their surroundings. Most preservation today is directed toward recycling older buildings and is motivated for financial as well as aesthetic satisfactions.

Preservation has become fundamental to city planning. No building can now be considered eligible for demolition and replacement until public and private expectations for the property have been investigated. Adaptive uses must satisfy the criteria of community groups with vested interests in the property to be rehabilitated. The costs of delaying a project while dealing with community resistance can diminish or eliminate profits.

Within historic districts there is frequently no choice but rehabilitation or adaptive use of existing structures. However, the amount of renovation activity outside as well as within these districts demonstrates that recycling old buildings is consistent with economic trends.

The square-foot hard costs of rehabilitation may not be lower than new construction, but the reduction in total time required for renovation, perhaps one year, as contrasted with two years for new construction, is frequently enough alone to justify a rehabilitation project as an alternative to new construction, considering the difference in carrying costs. Also the new tax benefits have been crucial in attracting capital to rehabilitation projects.

Many buildings can be rehabilitated at a lower cost than new construction although some can easily be replaced for less than their renovation cost. It all depends on the quality of the existing structure. When new construction of elevator office buildings can involve total costs between $100 and $200 per square foot, retrofitting a building may cost 25 to 50 percent less. In addition to savings in materials and time, labor costs have risen more slowly than the cost of materials and rehabilitation is more labor-intensive than new construction.

Adaptive use projects, however, have higher front-end technical evaluation and planning costs. One complication is that adaptive use involves the opposite of the ''form follows function'' principle which has for so long governed modern construction; adaptive use requires examination of existing space to see which functions it will accept. Developers must assess what facilities are in demand and which structures can be adapted in the most efficient manner to supply the market's needs.

The appraiser must make similar judgments. What is the highest and best use of the older property? What are the possible alternative uses? Must the integrity of the structure be preserved to maintain the income-earning potential of the building? Does the proposed renovation plan provide the required utility at a reasonable cost?

Adaptive use can proceed only where zoning regulations permit the new uses. Historic district zoning adds more constraints. Sometimes, however, zoning changes or exceptions are possible and the design review process required in historic districts is not necessarily a deterrent to rehabilitation. Improved tax revenues, increased employment, and the elimination of dilapidated structures are attractive incentives to city governments to change zoning regulations that may otherwise be roadblocks to change.

How is the highest and best use of an older property to be determined? Although many older buildings seem to be loaded with inutility as measured against their modern counterparts, their appeal to the market because of architectural style, charm, or history may more than offset the lack of total functional utility. However, in order to have market value, all buildings must possess usefulness and must therefore be acceptably functional.

Almost any kind of structure can be converted to offices, to retail stores, and to living space. Whether there is a demand for these uses in converted structures in a specific location is another matter. If there are already examples in the neighborhood, the appraiser must determine if these conversions are successful, and for what reasons. If there are no comparable examples, demand must be evaluated by the appraiser and the conditions delineated under which the building can meet the demand. Even though other projects have been less than totally successful or even outright failures, a superior conversion and renovation involving the same use may succeed although the risk is much greater than if a number of similar projects have been carried out successfully. On the other hand, once demand has been adequately met, one more project may be one too many.

The criteria for ascertaining the highest and best use of an adaptive use project are similar to those for determining the highest and best use of a vacant site, except that the functional limitations of the existing building may be excessively costly to overcome.

The method of ranking the alternative possible uses for an older structure is similar to the analysis of new construction: costs must be deducted from benefits. In the case of adaptive use projects, the income tax credits, preservation grants, ad valorem tax abatement, and the potential for preservation easement credits are widely available benefits that may be added to income or resale potential. It has been estimated that in the 2,500 National Register listings that are historic districts, as many as a million properties are eligible for donated preservation easements and the 25 percent investment tax credit. In addition there are properties in local historic districts that meet National Register criteria and also properties individually listed on the National Register. The 25 percent tax credit is available for all but owner-occupied residential structures; preservation easement deductions are available to all types of certifiable properties.

Renovation Costs

Although they are far less standardized, the costs of rehabilitating and adapting older buildings should be viewed with the same objectivity as new construction. The extent and nature of the renovation proposed may or may not constitute the most economic expenditure. Too little or too much expenditure may be planned; possibly the renovations are the wrong ones. Some rehabilitations of older structures must reverse "modernizations" such as the installation of aluminum window frames and lowered lay-in ceilings to capture the full potential of an historically or architecturally significant structure.

The use of renovation cost comparables will provide a balance in analyzing renovation cost as a contribution to market value. However, for some adaptive use projects, specific tax benefits or the availability of historic preservation funding are necessary to offset what would otherwise be noneconomic rehabilitation costs.

If a new use is not compatible with the characteristics of a particular old building, the cost of adaptation may not make economic sense or can delay the point at which profit will be available.

Undoubtedly, adaptive use will continue to evolve to meet the demands of the economy as construction technology has evolved in the past. Industries that manufacture and sell accurate replicas of moldings and other trim components, balustrades, windows, hardware, and lighting fixtures have developed, and a vigorous trade in architectural antiques has evolved.

Peripheral Considerations

Energy conservation is a significant component of the long-term trend to adaptive use. Every building in reasonable physical condition represents a stockpile of energy that can be conserved. Old masonry structures insulate against temperature changes; modern curtain wall construction makes much greater demands on heating and cooling systems. Window openings in older structures occupy a much smaller proportion of the exterior facades than in curtain wall buildings. Office buildings with windows that open provide insurance against power shortages that shut down mechanical cooling or ventilation.

Changes in architectural trends motivated by the need to conserve energy also affect residential development. Now being appreciated are houses with foot-thick brick walls: windows and verandahs provide natural air conditioning in the South; nearly windowless north walls provide insulation in colder regions.

Almost all new houses during the past decades were constructed with central heating and air conditioning. The careful siting, landscaping, and design that earlier had protected houses from the elements were not considered neces-

48

sary. As a result, American house architecture became homogenized. The rehabilitation of older structures has served as an example for the new construction industry in the area of energy conservation; once again new houses are being built to reflect regional and climatic characteristics, with unique aesthetic as well as practical appeal.

Although large cities are providing the more striking examples of adaptive use, the same trend is observable in smaller urban and rural areas. Main Streets, once so vital to sparsely populated areas of the U.S., then so neglected, are experiencing a minor renaissance. In the 1970s, for the first time in 160 years, population growth in the U.S. was higher in rural areas and small towns than in metropolitan areas.

Growth trends for major cities are ambiguous. The continuing out-migration of population to suburban areas is still stronger than the reverse trend. Auguring well for growth or at least stabilization of central cities, however, are the renovation of old housing stock, the revival of cultural resources, the boom in office building construction and downtown shopping facilities, and the expansion of downtown public transportation systems.

It has been predicted that more and more people will choose either to work near their homes or have their home and place of business within the same structure. The development of sophisticated communications and computer equipment and the escalation of energy costs will encourage this change. Such a trend could well encourage more adaptive use for some of the diversity of life will have to be provided by the immediate environment rather than by the movement from home to work. Chicago's two million square-foot Furniture Mart, now being converted into apartments, offices, and stores, illustrates how this can be accomplished on a grand scale.

Tourism has also spurred renovation and adaptive use. Groups of buildings that have been restored in some inviting natural setting such as a waterfront area attract visitors and create a demand for more shops, museums, restaurants, and lodgings. The revival of the small roadside inn is another aspect of the adaptive trend. These inns are as varied as the structures from which they are converted and as far in concept from the standardized chain hotel-motels as can be imagined.

Adaptive Uses—Great and Small

Many spectacular examples of adaptive use throughout the country have involved startling changes: shopping malls created out of factories, railroad stations, old movie houses, and trolley barns; piano factories becoming artists' studios; grain elevators and grist mills turned into apartments; churches made into restaurants and schools into office buildings. Mansions have become splendid professional offices. A dry goods store in Louisville was converted to a science museum; a bank in the same city became a theatre. In Denver an automobile dealership building is now a sporting goods store, ramps and all.

Some projects went against the economic tide before they were developed and, in some cases, for some time after. Some, like Underground Atlanta, have been failures in spite of early success. Other projects, like Ghirardelli Square, were prototypical: they set the stage and bore the brunt of the risk. Subsequent projects built upon their success. As with other types of real estate, no matter how clever or innovative and appealing, an adaptive use project can fail if it is in the wrong place at the wrong time. A large, architecturally attractive old brewery in a big city will make a wonderful shopping complex only if it is not physically isolated—unless it can regenerate a whole neighborhood by itself.

The start of the adaptive use movement can be traced to San Francisco, with its limited land supply. Even before the conversion of the Ghirardelli chocolate factory in the early 1960s, a multi-level ferry boat/parking garage across the bay in Sausalito, California, had quietly been converted into a shopping mall.

In 1967 Baltimore's Mt. Royal railroad station was remodelled as a school for the Art Institute. The station had been closed by the B&O Railroad in 1961 and sold to the Art Institute in 1964 for a nominal sum. The remodelling is a classic example of preserving the integrity of a structure while providing functional utility. Although renovation costs were kept under control, the low acquisition price at little more than land value made adaptive use possible where it otherwise might not have been.

A very beautiful and intriguing specialty shopping center, Georgetown Park, has been created on two sides of the C&O Canal in Washington, D.C.'s Georgetown out of a collection of old warehouses and stores. About 120 stores and restaurants surround a central skylighted atrium; the interior furnishings and fittings are Victorian in style. The upper levels of this project contain residential condominiums with views of the eighteenth century town, the Canal, and the Potomac River. The two sections are connected by two bridges over the Canal. The planning and execution that have gone into the project are extraordinary.

The challenge is to recognize the potential of under-utilized structures before the market in general does and to acquire the properties at prices permitting a profit after renovation. The market value of a property that is in little demand can move upward rapidly after developers have recognized a valid market potential by acquiring and appropriately renovating similar properties. The appraiser must judge the value of properties at various stages of recognized potential.

50

Special Benefits

The benefits of adapting older buildings to new or renewed uses go beyond federal tax credits and social fads. Architecture and structural integrity can reduce energy consumption; existing shells may exceed current zoning envelopes and thus provide added value. Furthermore, older buildings are frequently clustered in prime locations near public transportation modes, in which case an entire original development scheme can be recycled.

The most attractive prospects for development are structures with much of the original detail intact. By preserving the integrity and quality of these buildings, the developer can create a project with greater amenities than those possible with new construction. Concepts of functional utility have been altered by adaptive use projects. High ceilings are a benefit instead of a loss if they attract buyers or customers. Second-floor shops which might not survive in a newer building are often a success in a renovated older building. If shoppers come merely to shop efficiently they may avoid shops not immediately accessible from the street, but if they anticipate some entertainment in the form of interesting surroundings, they may be willing to make the effort to reach another level.

The attractions of waterfront redevelopment can profitably benefit other nearby development and replace obsolete shipping and warehouse functions. Art galleries, theatres, museums, and other cultural facilities are uses of grandly-proportioned older structures that add greatly to community life and encourage other real estate developments.

Special Problems

Building codes may be the single biggest stumbling block to successful recycling of old buildings. Fortunately, some cities have code provisions for historic structures and some have special appeal boards to handle the problems arising from the conflicts between building codes and adaptive use.

The fact remains that rehabilitation of an existing structure provides fewer design options than does new construction, despite structural integrity, quality of materials, attractive architecture, and energy conservation. Bearing walls, columns, hallways, and stairwells are very expensive or impossible to alter. Stringent building codes may require additional stairwells and emergency exits. In earthquake areas, renovation can require expensive seismic-protective alterations almost never included as a part of the original construction.

Generally, the less that is changed in a structure, the fewer code requirements that will have to be observed. According to most building codes, if a major portion of the building is to be changed, the renovation must conform to the building code in its entirety. Thus, building codes discourage changes of use.

There also is a limit to how innovative a developer should be. Although development should remain flexible, more and more real estate uses are subject to the fickleness of fashion, so that today's high rent producer may be tomorrow's cash drain. As with other types of real estate development, too many cute boutiques may produce an opposite reaction.

Nevertheless, almost any kind of structure has proved adaptable in an interesting fashion. The problem for the appraiser may well be to avoid being diverted by unique uses. Potential adaptive uses must be evaluated, just as new construction, in terms of the whole economic setting, considering income, expenses, costs, flexibility, utility, manageability, tax advantages, and resale value.

Not all buildings should be saved. Some are not adaptable; some have already surrendered their architectural integrity; some are physically depleted. Adaptive use may not be economic when a structure is far below the density permitted for the site, although in these cases donation of a preservation easement or the sale of development rights can help offset the loss of value. Whether a low-density improvement will be saved is a function of how historically or architecturally significant the structure is judged to be and what protection and subsidies are available. Partial demolition may be the most economic use of a structure; a few can be successfully enlarged without any serious compromise of integrity.

A New Professional Approach

As a new design ethic for interpreting existing structures has emerged and as the trend toward preservation and adaptive use has grown, the attitude of real estate professionals has become one of acceptance. Teams of experts in zoning, building codes and community preservation criteria have been formed to find and develop adaptable buildings; such a team might include an architect, an engineer, an architectural historian, a lawyer, an accountant, and a building contractor. An appraiser is required to make the team complete. The team must be able to: (1) make a structural and physical analysis of a building, alert to physical deficiencies that could prove too costly to correct; (2) conduct an architectural and historical evaluation, and (3) survey special funding resources and local and federal tax benefits. Appraisers on such teams must maintain their objectivity, which may be no more or less difficult than it is for appraisers to be objective in the face of the pressures associated with new construction projects.

As preservation activity has expanded, colleges and universities have begun to include preservation technology in their curricula; some have degree programs. These programs will usually include survey courses in the principles of preservation and specialized courses in archeological, architectural, museum, and archival technique. The remaining courses can be selected from related disciplines such as history, art history, and geography.

6

The Sales Comparison Approach

Valuing an historically significant, architecturally outstanding, or merely older structure, whether recently renovated or eligible for adaptive use, closely parallels the typical appraisal process; the difference lies in the need for an expanded awareness of the characteristics of older properties and the relationships of these characteristics to economic patterns.

The valuation process should move inexorably toward an objective value estimate. The process begins with delineation of the problem and an examination of the property's environment and its physical and historical characteristics. The process ends with the value conclusions developed in the various approaches, which are then correlated to a final conclusion. Other than for urban income-producing properties, the sales comparison approach generally will play a significant, if not the most important, role in the appraisal of historic and other older properties.

Comparison Characteristics of Historic Properties

In comparing sales of historic or architecturally outstanding real property, the added variables of age, complex architecture and construction, historic significance, and the greater disparities of deterioration and functional inutility must be considered.

Carrying out any appraisal is analogous to solving a mystery: the problem must be clearly understood, the facts assembled, the irrelevancies discarded, and the most probable solution derived through a logical process of analysis. The older the property, the more the potential for mystery. The date of construction and history of the property sometimes are not easily documented. The history of alterations and additions may be obscure. The uses to which older properties can be put and their income-earning capacity are much more subject to speculation than is the case for newer properties. The structural capacity and condition and the extent of physical deterioration may require the opinion of outside experts. Yet these mysteries must be solved.

Dates of original construction and major remodellings are desirable for sales comparisons. Some sleuthing among the local land records or at historic archives may be required to secure accurate dates for the appraised property and the comparables; public libraries often segregate historical data. Of major assistance will be any landmark lists that give dates and other characteristics.

If a property's background has already been described by an architectural historian, the Historic American Buildings Survey, or by some historic association, tracking down the date of construction and the history of the property will be relatively simple. Owners and others closely associated with a property often will have put together the most informed history available, including bibliographies of books and articles mentioning or detailing the property.

A description of the architectural style of the subject property and each comparable and its relationship to the date of construction are also desirable. Whether properties are typical or atypical of their date of construction can affect value. If a property is not typical, how does it differ? Authenticity, integrity, and typicality can be ascertained from reports of architectural historians, historic associations, state historic property offices, and such.

Some buildings combine varying architectural styles. The highest and best use of an historic property might include the removal of inharmonious components and the restoration of the original configuration and finish. However, some historic properties are prized because they demonstrate successive styles of architecture. All of the styles may be equally significant or one style may overshadow the others.

A property might also be associated with more than one event in history or more than one historic figure. For example, some buildings are associated with important events of both the Revolutionary War and the Civil War.

From time to time the waxing or waning of interest in a certain historic event, period, or person will produce changes in value for certain properties. Also a greater reverence for history seems to develop with the passage of time. The rarity of the oldest properties, particularly those of the seventeenth century, tends to produce the greatest potential for value enhancement.

Trends of this type should be evident from analysis of market data and should be increasingly easy to ascertain with experience in the appraisal of older properties. The comparison process essentially consists of isolating and analyzing as many variables as the appraiser considers influential in the marketplace. Units of comparison for older properties will still be those related to size, with adjustments for all of the other relevant variables.

Any type of historic designation of a property should be recognized in the appraisal process. The appraiser must understand the criteria for each designation, along with the accompanying benefits and penalties. There is a major difference between properties potentially eligible for investment tax credits or easement donations and those not eligible. The latter category includes properties not meeting the criteria for federal certification and those certified that have already taken advantage of all possible benefits. The differences should be given attention in the sales comparison process, for there will likely be a marked difference in demand.

The adaptability and functional utility of historic property are sometimes difficult to assess. Consider the rambling old mansion, now a semi-ruin, facing the sea. Could it become an attractive hotel? Much successful real estate development is the product of such creative thinking, tempered by practical considerations. Can the building be converted to a hotel for a reasonable sum of money without wrecking its character? Will the facilities that can be created be marginal, satisfactory, or excellent? The balance between practicality and romanticism essential in real estate entrepreneurship is nowhere more vital than in the development of historic properties.

Purists may wish to restore the mansion to its original condition as a house. But unless it is to be a public museum, it will likely remain a ruin, for it has obviously become uneconomic as a dwelling. Equally obvious is that the extreme practicalists who would replace the old mansion with a concrete box of a motel are also probably not recognizing the appropriate economic use of the existing structure. However, appraisers should examine the whole range of possibilities.

The practical aspects of adapting historic structures present many challenges. Can the extraordinary height of the old railroad station accept an intermediate floor level without losing its best feature? Will the extra staircase required by the building code cost too much and result in an unworkable floor plan? The comparison approach should give careful consideration to the adaptability and functional utility of all the properties involved.

Financing, zoning, and date of sale affect the prices of historic properties just as they do the prices of newer properties. All the more typical characteristics and motivational forces must be considered in the comparison process.

Appraisers should seek to reflect in their interpretations of historic significance the criteria of the marketplace. Historic properties do possess the potential for increased prestige of ownership, increased earning ability, and reduction of income or other taxes. Historic properties can also be burdensome, expensive to maintain, and economically anomalous to their surroundings. Where the highest and best use is demolition, but demolition is prohibited because of landmark designation, the market value of the property will be reduced, often greatly, as the increasing number of cases of arson involving designated properties attest. The appraiser's principal task, as always, is to relate the characteristics of the property to the criteria of the market.

Finding the Comparables

The appraiser's search for sales comparison data can result in too many comparables, too few, or perhaps none at all. Very rare or very old properties are troublesome in that so few properties are similar. There are also the unusual properties that occur singly, such as the only theater in town or the only inn in a rural area. These assignments require a market data search beyond the confines of the immediate locality.

The usual sources such as land records, computerized data, brokers and salespeople, and periodically published transactions can be used within the broadened market data search area, but there are other sources of assistance specifically for historic property. National publications such as *Preservation News* carry numerous listings of properties for sale in all parts of the country. Local preservation publications also carry listings of properties for sale. Following up on sales of properties listed in back issues can be productive. These listings and sales can also provide information about what features attract buyers most readily and what types of properties are available.

Real estate brokerage firms that specialize in large, expensive, or unusual properties or individuals who specialize in historic properties are potentially excellent sources of sales comparison data.

Some preservation society files on landmark properties include sale prices along with the history and detailed description of each sold property, date of sale, and buyers' and sellers' names.

Computerized data collections categorized by date of construction create the possibility of sorting out very useful data by stipulating, for instance, properties of one hundred years of age or more.

When the two differ, it is the subject property's highest and best use, rather than the use for which it was designed, that controls the selection of comparable sale properties. A building designed as a hotel but with a highest and best use as an apartment building should be compared primarily with apartment buildings, although hotels converted to apartment use would be even better.

A structure for which there are few local comparables can be compared in terms of its square footage and functional utility with other nonhistoric buildings. If, as in the case of an old theater, architectural merit is not present in the nearby comparables, that variable can perhaps be isolated and analyzed through comparison with other types of buildings that do possess architectural merit. If

58

no other buildings in the immediate surroundings have the degree of significance possessed by the subject property, the variable of historical significance or architecture should be analyzed through an expansion of the search area to other towns. As the market data area is broadened, the locational factors will become more variable, making direct comparison less certain. Nevertheless, with diligent effort a reasonable and logical analysis can be carried out for almost any property.

Relevant Economic Forces

Supply and demand meet at some point to create price or market value; decreased supply and/or increased demand will increase value in a free market and conversely, decreased demand and/or increased supply will decrease value. The supply of historic and rare architectural buldings is not susceptible to expansion as is the supply of new buildings. To satisfy the demands for interesting old buildings, a broader and broader delineation of what is historic has to some extent expanded the supply, and as time passes, more properties become historic, but there does remain a limit on the supply. Scarcity has driven up prices; properties with the greatest historical and architectural integrity rank at the top of this hierarchy.

There is some tendency for widespread imitations of traditional styles to decrease the demand for the authentic version. Potential buyers or users of property simply grow tired of seeing the repetitive imitations and seek out something different, if only a little different. This principle can apply to historical connotations as well as to architectural styles.

The principle of contribution should always be considered in the analysis of sales of historic properties. The cost of restoration, removal, or repair of deteriorated properties should be analyzed in relation to the contribution of the rehabilitation to the later value of the property. Costs should be weighed, not only against potential sale price and earning ability, but also against income and other tax benefits.

The sales comparison approach is certainly more complex for historic properties, but only rarely does it not provide a supportable indication of value.

7

The Cost Approach

The basic premise of the cost approach is that a property will sell at a price relative to a newly constructed version of itself. The cost to reproduce any commodity is a controlling element of value. Potential buyers and users automatically compare old buildings to new; the relative benefits and detriments of both are weighed and a judgment is made. Such judgments determine price and should be reflected by the appraiser.

Considering that historic significance cannot be reproduced, and much fine architecture is not likely to be, applying the cost approach to historic property may seem contradictory. However, because it embodies so well the principle of substitution, the cost approach is a useful approach to the value of older properties even though any historic element or extraordinary craftsmanship may be incremental to it.

The cost to put a property into proper condition for a potential use can be the major determinant of its feasibility. Estimating cost to rehabilitate is related directly to estimating cost new. The crucial question is how the increase in the value of the property will relate to the cost to rehabilitate.

The recognition of the amenities inherent in older properties can coexist in times of economic expansion with new construction, although poverty, it used to be thought, was the best preservationist. For many reasons already brought out here, the architecture and construction methods and materials of the past are now often preferred. Just a short time ago, this was hardly the case and many fine old structures were destroyed because new construction was considered a more economic use of the land. As a part of that pattern, many old buildings were demolished in the 1950s and the 1960s in the cause of "urban renewal" and these urban renewal areas became wastelands or were "improved" with what have subsequently been shown to be inferior structures. Certainly this has not always been the case, but sufficiently so that more caution is now usually exercised before existing buildings are demolished. There is in the post-urban-renewal era less of a clear-cut delineation as regards the most economic use of urban sites in the choice between new construction and preservation. This choice is, as always, related to cost. The cost to create the desired quality and character in a new building may be prohibitive. The relationship between construction cost and market value is best demonstrated by including a cost approach in the appraisal process.

Thousands of buildings within registered districts have little to recommend them from an historic standpoint apart from their location and streetscape contribution. Such historic districts were usually designated as part of the mushrooming "preservationist" movement which often promoted adaptive reuse, facade-only retention, recreations, and even imaginative new construction "inspired by" earlier buildings. This new industry has been responsible for many genuine restorations and has brought facsimiles within reach of the average home buyer. The movement has also imposed its will, through local governments, on the property of others. These factors are important within the context of the cost approach.

However, for the truly historic property, the cost approach is weakened by the fact that it is impossible to consider the reproduction cost of historical events associated with the building or to duplicate its conditions of construction; when it is these aspects that merit preservation the cost to replicate is not a method by which the market approaches value. An appraiser can, however, deploy the cost approach in several ways:

1. For the many properties that typify an average historic district—those with no peculiar historicity—a *routine cost approach* may be used much as it is for nonhistoric properties, i.e., replica cost, less deterioration and obsolescence, plus land value.

2. For buildings the highest use of which is major renovation (whether authentic restoration, adaptive use remodelling, or extensive rehabilitation including modernization), a *development cost approach* is often necessary, using the following steps to find the "as-is" value:
   a. Selection of the price level and type of renovation that is the highest and best use.
   b. Appraisal of the market value of the property on an "as renovated" basis by use of income capitalization, sales comparison, and/or summation.
   c. Subtraction of the likely renovation cost, defined here to include design, engineering, construction, legal, finance, in-

terest, and other project costs plus an entrepreneurial incentive.

3. The development cost approach indicates the maximum value of the unrenovated shell for investment purposes; the owner-occupant market may prefer the *modified cost approach* to reach the "as renovated" value: the renovation cost is added to the as-is price, the price for which a property was acquired, or the price at which it is available, by option or otherwise.

4. The *land valuation portion* of a cost approach is often necessary when appraising depreciable historic properties, particularly those eligible for rehabilitation tax credit.

5. A *residual cost approach* may be undertaken in the rare cases where it is necessary or desirable to isolate the relative degree of value increment that the market should consider.

This approach, for example, could be used to justify the "historic significance" adjustment made to comparables that, while similar locationally, chronologically, and physically, have dissimilar historicity or are associated with different events (Revolutionary War vs. Civil War) or persons (Franklin Roosevelt vs. Eleanor Roosevelt). This approach, while accurate for the *relative* difference, is not accurate for the finite difference unless the cost approach to value and the value *per se* are identical; yet no other technique is available for isolating the historic increment. The steps are as follows:

a. Select properties that have historic significance (without knowing whether the historic significance resulted in any increment, much less how much of an increment), and that sold under conditions known to the appraiser. (These properties need not be comparable to the appraised property; if they are, a sales comparison approach would probably be used instead of a cost approach.)

b. From each selected historic sale property's price subtract the appraised value of the land and the cost to replicate the building less the accrued deterioration and obsolescence. (All calculations are as of sale date.)

c. For each such sale divide the remainder by the price to produce the percentage increment.

Where actual reproduction of architectural components and original materials is required by historic district ordinances or by encumbering preservation easements, the cost of restoring or repairing a particular property may greatly exceed typical costs. Examples might include requirement to specially duplicate non-standard-sized bricks or individually cast terra cotta ornamentation. Appraisers need to ascertain whether such careful duplications are required and what their costs will be. Such extra cost constraints can significantly alter the economics of rehabilitating an historic property.

The income approach, paramount for most investment properties, is generally inadequate for owner-occupied properties, leaving only the cost approach to be balanced against the sales comparison approach in valuation. Historic properties may be worth much more than their cost new; the sales comparison approach used with the cost approach can demonstrate the increment for the historic factor.

All forms of depreciation are measured by the cost approach and all forms of depreciation affect the income and market approaches. Cost data can be the basis for adjustments in the other approaches. Deviations from cost-new also can be measured by sale price penalties and net income loss. The three approaches reinforce and complement each other; this desirable completeness should not be ignored when appraising older properties.

Applying the Cost Approach

Value is enhanced or reduced by surroundings. Any property must be appraised as part of its environment—the immediate neighborhood, and to a lesser extent, the community as a whole. The setting of an historical property should provide a degree of integrity. For instance, a plantation that 250 years ago consisted of 900 acres, but now consists of only 70, may still have integrity if the surroundings do not intrude on its rural serenity. Furthermore, 900 acres today would be an excessive site for this particular riverfront plantation property. On the other hand, if the gracious home of a renowned personage is now surrounded by office towers, a considerable measure of its historical integrity is lost.

The market value of historic properties located in a once prosperous environment that has since become economically distressed is more directly related to the site than to any historic distinction the buildings may possess. That the site itself is historic is a tenuous concept; the market does not always ascribe enhancement in value to the land under an historic structure. However, if an historic structure has been destroyed or removed, a higher price might accrue to the site if it might be redeveloped with a structure that reflects the historic improvements that once stood there or is related to the historicity of the site itself.

64

There are historic sites such as battlefields or ship landing sites that require no improvements to create their historicity. These sites also may have a higher value than the land surrounding them.

Sometimes historic structures that have become an inappropriate land use may be removable to another site. The more economic use of the site overshadows any historicity it may possess. Although the improvements have lost the integrity they had with the original site, they may contribute more in a new, more appropriate, setting.

However, other possibilities also should be considered:

1.   A restoration trend could cause the historic significance of the property to reemerge as a major determinant of value.
2.   The historic structure may enhance other, different, uses that are emerging.
3.   Anomalous historic structures can be protected "for the public good" through some form of subsidy.

Synergy almost always plays a part in the value of historical or older properties—where they are grouped, they tend to enhance one another; the total becomes greater than the sum of the parts.

Estimating Cost New

The estimation of cost new of older buildings naturally requires some knowledge of construction and architecture. Perhaps the dwindling popularity of the cost approach stems from the fact that many appraisers lack familiarity with these areas of expertise.

Construction techniques and skills to replicate and restore older buildings have emerged because the demand for them exists. Restoration or rehabilitation can be nearly as expensive as new construction of a more modern building or even more so, although generally there is a savings in the construction time required. New construction in the styles of earlier eras is not as unusual as it once was. Direct cost comparisons can usually be made for new construction, restoration, or rehabilitation, though an expert in cost estimation may be needed for unusual properties. In any case, the cost-new estimate cannot be expected to be exact; it need only be accurate enough to provide a reasonable basis for the cost approach conclusion.

In order to estimate cost new, accurate measurements and a floor plan must be ascertained. The relationship of usable area to gross area must be established.

The thick exterior walls of old buildings can cause a significant disparity between interior and exterior dimensions. Thick walls provide structural strength and longevity as well as protection from the elements and lowered energy consumption. Replacement cost based on a thin-walled structure will not reflect the value that a quality- and energy-conscious market would ascribe to such a building. Likewise, a clay-tiled roof will contribute a greater value than an asbestos-shingled roof (though perhaps not as great as the cost difference). On the other hand, a fire-resistant roof should probably be included in an estimate of the cost new of a building with a flammable roof. Appraisers do not need to guess at these choices; they can derive them from the actions of the marketplace. The cost new estimate may have to be a blend of reproduction and replacement cost based on the practicalities and preferences of the market.

There are frequently wide variations between the actual costs of similar projects, depending on the skill and experience of construction management and capability. Appraisers need to keep abreast of changing construction costs and technological advances that affect costs. Assembling cost data from more than one source insures a greater degree of accuracy in estimating cost new. National cost data services are very helpful, but need to be carefully weighed against the characteristics of the subject property and the actual project costs of similar properties.

Estimating Depreciation

Accurately estimating accrued depreciation in an older building can be a revealing, though demanding, task. Determining the actual physical condition of any structure, particularly an old one, can constitute a real challenge; the opinion of a structural engineer will sometimes be required. The threatened collapse of major structural components may not be apparent to the untrained observer. On the other hand, old buildings can settle into the earth, becoming neither plumb nor level, without any real structural damage. The aging process, in an initially well-built structure, can add to its attractions. However, if there is danger of serious damage to the components, some correction is required. Also modern electrical and plumbing systems are preferable over older ones that may be hazardous or inadequate. All systems should meet standards of safety as well as adequacy.

Insulation should be nonhazardous and installed so as not to interfere with adequate ventilation. Absolutely airtight buildings are subject to damp rot, mildew, and the production of toxic gases resulting from the deterioration of the insulation or other construction materials.

Uneven plaster and scarred woodwork may disturb the appraiser unaccustomed to the preferences of that segment of the market attracted to older properties. Plaster is difficult and expensive to replace; many prefer uneven plaster to drywall. Severely deteriorated plaster, however, may require replacement with a substitute, and for some purposes drywall may be the better choice. The appraiser must make a judgment as to such matters.

In general, older properties are rehabilitated to match the preferences of the market, and those preferences tend to include the preservation of traditional architecture and detailing rather than replacement with different elements. In installing the modern functional systems typical of rehabilitation of older buildings, care must be taken not to compromise architecture and interior finish with inappropriate lighting and plumbing fixtures and air conditioning vents.

With proper care and appropriate renewal or restoration, buildings can have physical lives of hundreds of years. The remaining economic life concept can be used to measure incurable physical depreciation, although the concept needs to be altered to reflect greater efforts to "cure" physical deterioration in old buildings. Similarly, cost to cure is an appropriate measure of curable physical deterioration.

Functional utility needs to be carefully considered in the cost-oriented analysis of older properties. A planned public showplace or museum that does not include incompatible additions or structures probably will not present any problems of functional inutility. Most older properties were designed to include what now is considered to be wasted space. Yet that space may be the very element that will attract the maximum income or price to the property. Again a considered judgment is necessary. The concept of usefulness or functional utility so central to market value is a major feature of the cost approach, which recognizes that a useless building contributes nothing to value, regardless of its cost new.

Some other items commonly considered elements of functional inutility may need to be reexamined. High ceilings, Victorian plumbing fixtures, wood sash windows, fireplaces, and lighting fixtures predating the 1950s are all sought after in certain types of markets, although compromises for practical purposes can be quite acceptable. Drastically lowered ceilings are consistently removed, but where air conditioning is required, the ductwork has to go somewhere. Fireplaces, attractive though they may be, are inefficient in terms of energy consumption and heat retention unless they are appropriately retrofitted.

Functional utility considerations should include comfort, security, convenience, light and air, pride of ownership, attractiveness, reasonable maintenance expenditure, and the preservation of tradition. Functional utility is not always exemplified by minimal space or form. Some inconvenience can be offset by charm, beauty, or rarity.

The physical integrity of a property with historical or architectural significance should be a consideration in the analysis of its accrued depreciation. If few original components remain, the cost of restoration of the structure could exceed its market value restored; the disparity is functional inutility, and can be measured by sales of similar properties.

Functional utility is not a finite concept; it is always subject to changing standards. Functional inutility or obsolescence is defined as impairment of functional capacity or efficiency; but the appraiser must judge it within the context of market standards of the buyers who make up the market for the particular category of building.

Incompatibility is another element of depreciation to be considered; it can be classified as economic obsolescence. To be compatible, buildings must be in harmony with their environments and uses. This harmony should extend to form, materials, and scale. Compatibility, however, is a less regimented concept than conformity.

To sum up, the cost to build new, less depreciation, plus land value, can be very useful in determining what to pay for existing properties if depreciation is estimated accurately. Physical deterioration and curable functional obsolescence can readily be measured by the cost to cure; incurable physical deterioration, if any, can be measured by the age life concept or by using income or sales data from the marketplace. Incurable functional and economic obsolescence are also measured by income and sales data. There are generally sufficient sources of cost and depreciation data in any market.

Concluding the Cost Approach

In assembling the component parts of the cost approach, property should be valued on the basis of consistent use, not on one use for the land and another for the improvements.

Entrepreneurial profit must be given proper consideration; construction is motivated by this profit, even when a property is owner-built for owner occupancy. Entrepreneurial profit is incremental to the total of all direct and indirect construction costs.

Once the depreciated building contribution has been added to site value the appraiser's judgment as to any increment attributable to historicity or outstanding architecture can be added. This increment should be derived from sales or income data available from the market.

Insurable value is a particular problem where historic properties are concerned. Replacement cost, on which insurable value is commonly based, cannot adequately recognize the uniqueness associated with historically or architecturally significant structures. An historically significant building may have a contributory value well above the cost to rebuild its replica. A greater-than-cost policy can be difficult to purchase. Policies must be carefully drawn to eliminate language that would limit casualty partial loss to physical replacement where that amount is below the cost of economic replacement.

8

The Income Approach

The income approach is based on the relationship between the various future income benefits of ownership and current sale prices in the open market. Anticipated income benefits include security of payment, amount and duration of payment, and the extent to which income is taxable. Buyers anticipate these benefits partly on the basis of current net income earned and partly on the basis of expected changes. Together, current net income and tax shelter and the expectation of future net income and tax shelter establish the relationship between income and sale price. Even those properties of limited income potential demonstrate a relationship between income expectations and market value. Appraisers use the income approach to discern and interpret these patterns.

Many historic properties are single-family residential properties. These are seldom acquired for income considerations and the income approach has little applicability to their valuation. Their historicity may greatly enhance their potential for appreciation and consequently they may be viewed by the market as excellent investments. Other historic properties that have both potential for appreciation and modest income potentials can be valued effectively by income analysis combined with the other approaches; these will demonstrate very low overall rates because their potential for value enhancement stems partly from characteristics other than net income production. However, income analysis becomes crucial for the many historic properties with income production capacity that are being rehabilitated on the premise of a competitive income return.

Many properties with historic or architectural significance have significant income potential. Historic properties attract grants, subsidized financing, and other kinds of public sponsorship. The investment tax credits for rehabilitation of older properties and the potential for preservation easement donations have substantially enhanced the investment position of historic properties. The majority of older properties classified as historic are investment properties for which the income approach is a principal measure of value. Analysis of the rent, expenses, capitalization rates (or internal rates of return), and tax benefits of these properties is the primary approach used by investors and, consequently, one that should be applied in the appraisal process.

How Much Income?

Many of the monumental historic structures in the United States are owned and managed by federal, state, and municipal governments. These buildings, including the White House, the Library of Congress, state capitols, courthouses, libraries, and museums, rarely require appraisal, although occasionally a rental or a value has to be estimated. Monumental buildings are less likely to have limited economic lives; they are more likely to be focal points around which more speculative development comes and goes. The upkeep of these buildings is almost certainly assured and their value is likely to appreciate. Expenses for maintenance and utilities are high, in line with their public use and their value to the public. Though rental value is likely to be commensurately high, equivalent dollar income is almost always severely negative; yet, they remain very valuable.

Rentals for publicly owned, monumentally scaled, properties may need to be established as the basis for appropriations. Also, these properties, although rarely sold, may require appraisal for transfer from one governmental agency to another. Where the use is one commonly producing rent such as office use, the income approach may be the principal measure of market value. In estimating the appropriate income and expenses, the appraised property can be compared with properties of similar usefulness and appeal. Operating expenses for utilities, cleaning, and maintenance, for monumentally scaled buildings may contribute to higher-than-typical occupancy costs because of operating hours, ceiling heights, and foot traffic. If these expenses are included in the estimated rents attributed to the buildings it becomes clear why they are publicly owned and subsidized.

When appropriate, a market-equivalent expense estimate can be substituted for the actual experience. Publicly-owned buildings are less likely to suffer from depreciation than speculative ones; they tend to set the standards rather than being competitively threatened by new construction. Capitalization rates used against projected income streams should reflect the nonwasting asset quality of monumental buildings as well as their lack of competitive risk.

Other first-rank historic properties, open to the public but owned privately, may also require appraisal services. Usually these properties can no longer be used for the purposes for which they were designed because of economic changes. Many have been restored or retained in their original condition and opened to the public as museums. Such properties are frequently owned by nonprofit organizations that benefit from their tax-exempt status and their ability to attract volunteer labor as well as visitor fees, donations, legacies, grants, and widespread public support, although income levels may be lower than those of a more typical investment property. Their income-generation and expense-reduction benefits are directly related to the market value of the property. The expenses that would otherwise have to be deducted from the gross income can be greatly reduced for a museum quality historic property by exemptions from taxation and volunteer labor.

In addition to the potential for income and expense reduction of these properties, their historic status further provides them with the prospect, like fine art, of growing ever more valuable. The resulting elimination of the need for capital recapture and the assurance of value appreciation allows the capitalization of their net income at very low rates relative to those appropriate for other properties. These properties are likely to have more income but less value than the monumental government properties. Again the rate of yield or of capitalization is the relationship between income and value.

The Second Tier

The second tier of historic properties includes those of significant landmark status that are privately owned, have not been converted to museums, and for economic reasons, landmark zoning controls, or easement encumbrances, generate only limited income. Economic reasons might be related to poor location,[1] deterioration or limited functional utility. Some of these may be curable but in concert with landmark zoning controls or easement encumbrances may be infeasible. Tax credits for rehabilitation do not always offset the obstacles.

For many properties, the public focus on historicity is a real detriment in terms of income potential. The income approach can reveal the relationship of the income streams of these properties to market value and isolate specific income-earning deficiencies.

Competitive Income-Earning Historic Properties

The broadest tier of historic real estate is made up of those older properties that can produce a competitive income stream. The return produced by these properties may be augmented by tax benefits, local tax reduction or moratoria, sub-

---

[1]Location is very important; were Mount Vernon further from Washington, D.C., its huge visitor-fee income might be much, much lower.

sidized financing, or grants. The tax reduction features of certifiable historic properties makes them particularly attractive to investors seeking tax shelter.

Ownership of these historic properties is frequently in partnerships or joint ventures with the investors sharing the tax shelter; larger historic properties are sometimes structured as public offerings. The development and use of this category of historic properties is an active segment of the real estate market stimulated by a multitude of factors including energy shortages, the reluctance or inability of local jurisdictions to provide new public improvements, tax and other government incentives, and changes in the interests and preferences of the public. Once the special benefits have been exhausted by a generation of ownership, these properties may not continue to be competitive.

Durrell Park: A Case in Point

An example will illustrate some of the differences in application of the income approach between historic properties and their newer counterparts. Durrell Park is a small shopping mall being created out of two-story-and-basement Victorian buildings in an urban neighborhood that is experiencing a rehabilitation trend. The structures, constructed in 1885, are typical commercial buildings of that period, now quite dilapidated. The owners have received federal certification of these buildings as contributory to the historic district in which they are located. The owners have also received preliminary certification of the rehabilitation program that has just begun. This work will cost approximately $1,700,000 including all direct and indirect costs. There are 24,000 square feet of gross building area, 8,000 square feet on each of the three levels. The basement is partially above grade and will have attractive terraced entrances tied in with the landscaping. A restaurant with an outdoor cafe is to be the major basement tenant. The investment in the property is as follows:

Acquisition Cost	@ $29.17/sf =	$ 700,000
Direct Rehab Cost	@ $50.00/sf =	1,200,000
Indirect Costs	@ $20.83/sf =	500,000
Total Out-of-Pocket	@ $100.00/sf =	$2,400,000

Contract rents for similar developments nearby indicate the following level of projected income for Durrell Park:

First Floor	6,400 sf @ $21.87 =	$140,000
Second Floor	7,600 sf @ $17.76 =	$135,000
Basement	7,000 sf @ $12.86 =	$ 90,000
Total	21,000 sf @ $17.38 =	$365,000

The rents projected assume that tenants will pay for their own cleaning and utilities. The leases will provide for annual escalation tied to the Consumer Price Index and for overage rent. Tenants will also pay for increases in real estate taxes above the first year's base level. Based on the experience of similar projects, the expenses of operating the project are stabilized as follows:

Item	Annual Amount	$/sf (21,000 sf)
Collection Loss and Vacancy	$ 5,000	$ .24
Management	10,000	.48
Real Estate Taxes	30,000	1.43
Insurance	5,000	.24
Trash Removal and Landscaping	5,000	.24
Electricity	1,500	.07
Water	2,000	.09
Repairs and Maintenance	15,000	.71
Miscellaneous	1,500	.07
Total	$75,000	$3.57

The stabilized expenses, including vacancy and collection loss, are 20.6 percent of projected gross rent, producing a stabilized net income of $290,000. Lease provisions will likely cause this rent to increase year by year, but there is no certainty of increase. Nevertheless, the appropriate capitalization rate for such an income stream is one that accurately reflects the relationship between present value and the anticipation of future benefits.

The overall rate of return, considering net income and out-of-pocket investment, in the project is 12 percent. A *cost* approach to value would call for the addition of an entrepreneurial incentive; a typical 15 percent of the rehabilitation cost would bring a cost approach to a total of $2,655,000, of which the net income of $290,000 is 10.92 percent.

The cost of financing as of the date of appraisal is competitive: a 70 percent-of-value loan will require a mortgage constant payment of 15 percent (debt service of $278,775), mandating a 10.5 percent overall rate mortgage component. The equity income is $11,225 or 1.4 percent of the $796,500 equity investment. The equity income is less than four percent of total income; this amount of leverage endangers the project. Yet the developer has assembled a group of investors eager to share in ownership. Even the mortgage lender (relying on a discounted cash flow, year-by-year, projection that predicts income increases and regular appreciation in the value of the property) is willing to make the loan, at 70 percent of the $2,655,000, even though the stabilized net income of $290,000 provides a debt coverage ratio of only 1.04.

Assuming that the rehabilitation receives final certification from the Department of the Interior and that all of the rehabilitation costs can be capitalized, the owners may deduct 25 percent of the rehabilitation costs from their income taxes. Because the credit is a deduction from taxes owed rather than a deduction from gross income to determine taxable income, it does not matter what tax bracket the owners are in; each dollar of credit results in a dollar of tax saving. Furthermore, only 50% of this investment tax credit has to be deducted from the depreciable basis of the property. If the property is held for five years the tax credit is not subject to recapture. Coupled with a straight-line depreciation schedule for the whole basis in the property plus the cost of rehabilitation, the investment tax credit can be a windfall or can wholly or in part offset an otherwise less than competitive income-earning potential.

For Durrell Park, the investment tax credit provides for an immediate recapture of one-quarter of $1,700,000 or $425,000, assuming the investors have equivalent income tax obligations. Adding $425,000 to the $2,655,000 result of the cost approach produces a total value of $3,185,000 and the overall rate that results from this and the stabilized net income of $290,000 is 9.11 percent. In this case 53 percent of the equity of $796,500 is repaid the first year via the tax credit.

If investors are purchasing similar properties that lack certifiable historic status at overall capitalization rates ranging around 10.92 percent, the historicity of Durrell Park has apparently reduced the overall rate by 1.81 percent. Not all owners can take advantage of the investment tax credit, so a 9.11 percent overall rate does not necessarily apply to the property unless the "typical" buyers of the definition of market value can benefit fully from the tax credit. The rates are further reduced by the tax shelter afforded by the mortgage interest deduction and the capital recapture provision allowance.

Other factors could offset the reduction in the overall rate: not all of the rehabilitation costs may qualify; some may reflect new construction instead of rehabilitation. However, new construction that is necessary to protect the integrity of an historic structure can be eligible for the tax credit.

If the rehabilitation work does not meet the Secretary of the Interior's Standards for Rehabilitation, the certification will be denied unless the deviations can be corrected. The property must have been in use for at least 20 years prior to the rehabilitation program, 75 percent of the original walls must be retained, and the cost of the rehabilitation must be equal to the depreciable basis in the property, or $5,000, whichever is lower. Indirect costs are mostly eligible for inclusion; these include architectural and engineering fees, real estate commissions, site survey fees, legal expenses, insurance premiums, developer's fees, and construction interest and fees.

9

Preservation Easements

Introduction

The term *preservation easement*, as used here (also called a covenant, restriction, or servitude) includes what are variously called historic, open space, scenic, conservation, and facade easements. An easement, as a nonpossessory partial interest in a property, can be deeded away, under federal legislation, to properly qualifying nonprofit organizations or government agencies, with an income tax reduction accruing to the donor. The income tax deduction can be equal to, but may not exceed, the market value of the real estate rights donated. The motivation to donate may be either a reduction in income taxes, the protection of historic or scenic property, or both.

The valuation of preservation easements is a new concept in the appraisal field, although the underlying economic theory is generally the same as that which governs eminent domain appraising, despite that the acquirer receives rights rather than taking them and the property owner gives them rather than having them taken. Each easement document is an individual set of controls and restrictions and should be so considered by the appraiser. The deed of easement must be carefully analyzed to determine its effects on the encumbered property. The level of controls of historic district or individual landmark designations, if any, should be related to the subject property and to the provisions of the easement.

The major objective of the preservation easement legislation is protection of properties through the prohibition of certain physical changes, usually based on the condition at the time of the donation of the easement, or immediately after a proposed restoration. Most of the specifications of preservation easements are negative, limiting or forbidding change. Prohibition of neglect is usually stated as a positive requirement for maintenance. Some easements also specify positive restoration work. The easement is created by a deed of easement; the donee must be a government entity or a properly qualifying nonprofit organization.

The potential decrease in value attributable to an easement is usually counterbalanced by historic district zoning, though this depends on the enforceability and the stringency of the legal controls of the district.

History of Preservation Easements

The enabling federal tax law is Internal Revenue Code Section 170, which provides for a donation of an easement, a lease, an option to purchase, or a remainder interest, in perpetuity, for conservation purposes, to a nonprofit organization or a government body. Before the 1976 Tax Reform Act, whether a preservation or conservation easement constituted an undivided interest in a property, as was required, was unclear. However, in 1964 a Revenue Ruling had permitted deduction of the value of a restrictive easement donated to the United States government in perpetuity. The Tax Reform Act of 1969 restricted deductions for income, estate, or gift tax purposes to transfers of the entire interest in a property, with several exceptions, one of which was an undivided interest in the property. The Conference Report on the 1969 Act stated that a gift of an open space easement in gross and in perpetuity was to be considered a gift of an undivided interest. The income tax regulations were modified in 1972 to include specific recognition of the deductibility of gifts of open space easements.

The Tax Reform Act of 1976, as part of the historic preservation and conservation tax incentives (Section 2124), provided more explicitly for a charitable deduction for donations of easements than any previous legislation. The donation of a lease, option to purchase, easement, or remainder interest was clearly stated to be an exception to the law which disallowed deduction for the donation of a partial interest. The 1976 Act specified charitable deductions for easements that were exclusively for "conservation purposes," to include "historically important land areas or structures"—a phrasing that permitted broad interpretation. These provisions were enacted with a sunset date of 1981; they were extended permanently by the Tax Treatment Extension Act of 1980.[1] As currently enacted, a qualifying easement donation must be for the protection of (1) land areas for public outdoor recreation or education, (2) scenic enjoyment or natural environmental systems, or (3) historically important land areas or structures. The latter category is defined as any building, structure, or land area that: (1) is listed in the National Register, (2) has been certified by the Secretary of the

---

[1] Pub. L. 96-547.

78

Interior as being of historic significance to an historic district listed on the National Register, or (3) is in an historic district certified as meeting the criteria of the National Register.

Significant guidelines for valuing preservation easements were contained in the *Thayer* decision of 1977 (T.C. Memo 1977-370), involving a country estate in Virginia with potential for subdivision into residential lots. The owner donated a preservation easement on the property to the Virginia Outdoors Foundation, prohibiting subdivision, timber cutting, commercial or industrial uses, signs or outdoor advertising and construction of any but farm buildings. The IRS contested the deduction. Both sides presented appraisal testimony at the trial; both witnesses agreed that the highest and best use of the property *after* the easement was granted was continuance as a country estate; however, they disagreed as to highest and best use before the easement. The appraiser for the owner recognized a potential for subdivision into a number of residential lots; the appraiser for the government testified subdivision was precluded for reasons of limited access, difficult topography, and sewer problems.

The single issue in contention was the amount of the deduction. The court found that the highest and best use before imposition of the easement was subdivision, but into a lesser number of residential lots than had been determined by the owner's appraiser. The Thayer decision affirmed the need for two appraisals: (1) of the property before the easement and (2) of the property encumbered by the easement. Although many issues regarding preservation easements and their valuation remained untested, the Thayer case establishes that competent appraisals are required. The final decision was that the easement reduced the value by 32.5 percent or 37.7 percent, depending on whether the taxpayer's appraisal or the IRS appraisal is accepted as the before-easement market value.

The Easement as a Deduction from Taxable Income

The donation of a preservation easement provides shelter for ordinary income that is not subject to any kind of tax recapture. There is a minor limitation: if the total of all itemized charitable donations, including a preservation easement, exceeds 60 percent of the taxpayer's adjusted gross income, the excess becomes a preference subject to additional minimum tax. The donation of an easement reduces the donor's depreciable basis in the property if it decreases the value of the improvements; in fact, the basis can be reduced to zero. The entire value diminution of both land and building attributable to the easement can be deducted; the amount of depreciable basis does not limit the amount of the deduction that can be taken.

There is a limit of 50 percent of the taxpayer's adjusted gross income that can be taken in any one year; however, if the value of the gift exceeds these limits, it can be carried forward over the five succeeding years. If the property has increased in value since it was acquired by the donor (capital gain) the deduction is limited to 30 percent of the adjusted gross income in the year of the gift; but, again, the balance can be carried forward for five years. If a property has been held for less than one year, the proportion of the easement value that can be deducted is diminished.

In spite of these limitations, the potential for income tax reduction by gifts of preservation easements is generally greater than for other tax-reduction incentives. The gift of an easement shelters a very large percentage of a donor's taxable income over a period of as much as six years; it also reduces capital gains tax at the time of a sale and reduces estate and gift taxes. Tax savings are, of course, limited to the amount of the total tax on a donor's income before the easement donation; therefore, the value of a preservation easement is of more importance to the donor with a greater tax liability.

Preservation Easements in the Marketplace

The major premise underlying preservation easement tax reductions is that the value of property so encumbered is diminished. An encumbrance that transfers rights in a parcel of real estate to another entity cannot fail to affect the encumbered property, though understanding of the effects may not be immediate. Some properties, especially those with a highest and best use that includes immediate demolition or new construction, are obviously greatly diminished in value by imposition of a preservation easement. On the other hand, negligible value loss may accrue to properties with a developed density equal to (or greater than) that permitted by current zoning, and with acceptable architecture and functional utility for an economic use. Where developed use is the most economic use of the land, the preservation easement will have only a minor effect at the time of donation.

However, because circumstances change, over the long term the requirement to maintain the status quo through economic conditions that contraindicate maintenance may become onerous for the property owner. Knowledgeable buyers will likely recognize this. And many potential buyers would not want to own a property for which the conditions of ownership are dictated by some outside entity. The market value should be penalized to the extent the appraiser believes the market will recognize these effects. Only a misinformed buyer would purchase a property encumbered with a typical preservation easement at a price equivalent to that which he or she would pay for an unencumbered property otherwise equal. Moreover, once a property is encumbered with an easement, it is no longer eligible for donation; a new buyer cannot take advantage of the potential for tax reduction.

Type of Restrictions

A preservation easement may include the following provisions:

1. Prohibition of all subdivision or a specific subdivision.
2. Prohibition of partial or total demolition.
3. Prohibition of all additions, or only those visible from the street.
4. Prohibition of any change to the physical appearance of the improvements or a part or parts of the improvements. Usually minor changes can be made with the written approval of the donee; even changing the paint color requires this written approval.
5. Prohibition of any increased density of use.
6. Prohibition of excavation or other topographical changes.
7. Prohibition of tree removal or other changes to the landscaping.
8. Prohibition of change of use or of certain uses.
9. Limitation or prohibition on advertising (signs, billboards, show windows).
10. A requirement to maintain the existing physical condition or an altered or improved physical condition.
11. A requirement to permit regular inspections.
12. A requirement that the property be open to the public during specified time periods.

The highest and best, or most economic, use of the property may be altered radically, slightly, or not at all, by these requirements. The highest and best use of the property will change in time; a major impact of most easements, whether or not it is recognized at the time of donation, is the loss of the flexibility to conform the property to the inevitable economic trends.

Another major area of impact is the loss of the traditional property rights that include using and changing the property according to personal preference. The appraiser should interpret each provision of the easement: Does the loss of excavation rights mean no swimming pools? Can air conditioning or energy-saving features be added? The appraisal should be conditioned on the assumption that the appraiser's interpretations are correct and that the deed of easement will conform to the stated provisions. If the easement has already been donated and the deed recorded, the assumptions can be confined to the appraiser's interpretations of the recorded easement.

Appraisal Methodology—Before and After Appraisals

The two-appraisal process is not required; however, precedent has established it as appropriate and acceptable. Again, the economic theory involved is consistent with eminent domain appraisal methodology. If the sale of preservation easements should become commonplace, valuation through direct comparison with sales of other easements would, of course, constitute a superior approach.

Valuation of the property before imposition of the easement must carefully consider the most economic use of the property as of the appraisal date. The potential for subdivision, for demolition and redevelopment, for renovation, and for altered use and occupancy should be analyzed in view of the current market. The contribution to total value of such components as (1) land and building, (2) subdividable land and land retained with improvements, or (3) improvements that should be demolished and those that should be retained, etc., should be established within the context of the before-easement appraisal as a basis for the diminutions or enhancements that will result from the easement.

After the easement, the highest and best use of the property is dictated by the terms of the easement. Some of the conditions of the easement may have dramatic effects on the market value of the property; others may have none. The conditions should be carefully analyzed for both individual and cumulative impact.

Valuation by All Three Approaches

Both before and after valuations can be accomplished by whatever combination of cost, sales, or income analysis is appropriate. The cost approach is helpful, in that it isolates the land and building components. Income analysis provides recognition of the variations in income, expense, and return on investment expectations caused by easements given in perpetuity. Direct comparison with sales is the best approach to the valuation of the land and replaces or supports the other approaches, depending on the type of property. One approach or more may be useful but none should be totally neglected. All values estimated should be supported by the actions of the marketplace, not contrived.

The Cost Approach

The cost approach, because it is a summation, separates the land and building components that are integrated in the income and sales data approaches. It is generally necessary for the sake of clarity to identify land value loss as a separate component; this is best done within the context of before- and after-easement land value. The building component, both as related to cost new and as a residual component of the whole property value, can be enhanced as the land value is diminished. Also, the cost to restore or rehabilitate a building may have to be developed so that it can be deducted from an estimate of value as rehabilitated in order to estimate the value of the shell building with its site either in lieu of, or in addition to, estimating the as-is value by direct comparison.

Valuation of the Land

Land value has an integrity or completeness apart from any improvements. Land as a component of total property value is considered as though vacant. The value of land beyond the purposes of agriculture and recreation lies in its potential for development with structures that provide shelter or income; this potential is controlled by its proximity to other development and by the police powers, such as zoning, exercised by the jurisdiction.

Because land is valued independent of improvements, land value can exceed total property value, when the improvements constitute a penalty, or can be the major proportion of the value, when new development is economically indicated. Preservation easements negate changes in the development of encumbered land. If the land component is all or most of property value before imposition of the easement, the easement may greatly diminish the value of the property. Nevertheless, the value of the easement may not be as great as the diminution in land value, because frequently building contribution to value increases post-easement. If the highest and best use before the easement requires the demolition of the improvements and the easement restricts such development, the after-easement value will probably include an intensified improvement contribution.

Properties improved with buildings functionally obsolete in terms of the highest and best use of the land are excellent candidates for preservation easements for two reasons that are really one: (1) they, more than others, need protection if they are worthwhile landmark properties, and (2) the values of easements on this type of property tend to be substantial. In other words, the value of the preservation easement is greater if the best use is demolition than if the best use is preservation.

Valuation of the land both before and after the easement can generally be accomplished through direct comparison or, failing the availability of comparables, through a residual process. Pre-easement, the highest and best use is established by the actual zoning or development potential, as evidenced by nearby development; post-easement, development is limited in perpetuity to the density represented by the extant improvements. Even when catastrophe results in partial or total destruction of the improvements, the encumbered density governs; most easements state that in case of partial or total destruction only a building of equivalent height and bulk can be reconstructed.

Land sale comparables permitting a density of development equivalent to that of the existing improvements can be useful in after-easement land valuation if their locations are similar; or land value can be determined using the same comparables as in the before-easement valuation, reducing the value in proportion to the loss in density potential. A pro-rata reduction may not be appropriate; the lower floors of any potential development project may contribute more to value than higher floors. For example, if a preservation easement reduces the density permitted from the building-to-land ratio of 10:1 (a 10.0 Floor Area Ratio) stipulated by the zoning to the ratio of 2.5:1 that the improvements represent, a density of 7.5 is lost. If the land has a value, as established by sales comparison, of $300 per square foot or $30 per square foot of permitted new construction, it does not necessarily follow that the value of the land after imposition of the easement is exactly $75 per square foot (at $30 per square foot of FAR), although roughly this is probably so. The loss of the upper floors of development potential should be valued on the basis of their individual contribution to value. Upper floors may, in fact, contribute more to land than lower floors, but the first floor often has the potential for the greatest contribution and, of course, below-ground rights, not in the Floor Area Ratio, also contribute value.

In addition to the lost potential development rights that are the difference between the zoning envelope and the density of the existing building, keeping the existing building may produce a land value penalty resulting from the functional inutility of the existing building as compared with potential new construction. For example, the efficiency of the rentable area as a percentage of gross building area for an older building will likely be lower than what could be achieved within the same envelope with new construction. Capitalized rent loss can measure this diminution; land value can also be related to rentable as well as to gross square feet of building to ascertain the appropriate penalties.

Easements that prohibit additions or extensions to existing improvements can result in significant penalties to land value where enlarging the building constitutes a more economic use. Some easements prohibit only extensions that are visible from the street. In these cases the penalty may be lessened or eliminated depending on whether an addition at the rear is physically possible or economically feasible.

Even though the property is within an historic district in which architectural

84

changes are controlled, additions, alterations, and even demolition may be permitted, albeit after review, and excess land can generally be developed with compatible structures. The controls as they are administered in the landmark district or in relation to the individual landmark property must be weighed against the controls imposed by the easement. When demolition and immediate redevelopment are not the highest and best use and there is no potential for increasing the development density by enlarging the building, there still may be a measurable diminution in land value if the improvements have a short economic life remaining. For example, assume that the zoning of a property permits construction of 40-story office buildings and this type of development is taking place in nearby neighborhoods, although there is no new construction in the immediate location of the property and there are no sales or vacant sites. The appraiser concludes that new office construction will reach the subject location within five years. If the subject property is in a landmark district, new office building development will have to proceed elsewhere, but if the property is an individual landmark, the easement can cause it to become completely anomalous to the neighborhood by the end of the five-year period.

The land value loss can be calculated as the present worth of the lost development density, deferred for the period of the remaining economic life of the improvements. Assume sales of vacant sites acquired for immediate redevelopment in the nearest neighborhood with the same zoning are at $800 per square foot, or $20 per square foot of potential new building. The subject building is developed to an FAR of 10. The difference in FAR of 30 indicates a loss of $600 per square foot of land at today's sale prices that is not available to the subject property for five years. The $600 deferred for five years has a present worth of about 50 percent or $300 per square foot discounted at 14 percent. A higher discount rate would produce a smaller loss and a lower rate a greater one; in any case, the discount rate is derived from the market's expectations for five-year investments. This land value loss, like the others discussed here, may be offset by building-value enhancement.

If direct comparison is precluded as a methodology for land valuation by a lack of available data, a residual approach may be indicated. Or both direct comparison and residual analysis can be used. In any case, the speculative profits to be gained through development are not a proper addition to land value loss. The measurement of loss is the difference between the prices the vacant land would bring in the open market before the easement and after the easement.

If the reduction in the development density or residential land specified by the easement is in terms of dwelling units—the land is limited to one house per acre rather than the five permitted by the zoning—the land has a potential for X dwelling units in the before-easement valuation and for X-Y units in the after-easement valuation. Adjustments to the prorata reduction should reflect whether the lower number of dwelling units results in some offsetting enhancement because of more open space, or a further penalty because of increased grounds-care expense.

If the highest and best use of residential property is not demolition of existing improvements but includes subdivision of land not required to support the improvements, the land value diminution should reflect loss of the subdivision rights. Subdivision potential will be demonstrated by nearby development and there will be a disparity between prices paid for land with this potential and prices paid for otherwise equally desirable land with little or no subdivision potential. This price difference separates the before-easement and after-easement land valuation. For example, land that sells for $5,000 per acre on the edge of a subdivision and $2,000 per acre further from development demonstrates the effect on land of an easement prohibiting subdivision.

Land value loss extends to the lost potential for sale of less than legal development lots to adjacent owners who can make profitable or desirable use of the land. This type of valuation can also be best carried out through direct comparison with sales of vacant land. For post-easement valuation, data can be assembled to demonstrate the diminishing contribution of the excess units of land.

The Income Approach

When the most economic use of a landmark property eligible for an easement donation is demolition, the value of the land is higher than the value of the property by the income approach. Income capitalization is necessary to support the appraiser's conclusion of most economic use, especially when some ambiguity attends the juxtaposition of the results of the valuation of the property by direct comparison with improved sales and the valuation of the land considered as vacant. When, on the other hand, the highest and best use before the easement is maintenance of the improvements, the result of the income approach will be supported by the results of the other approaches. A highest and best use that involves renovation can be demonstrated by income capitalization as renovated, deducting the cost of renovation. The result will indicate whether or not there is a building contribution beyond the value of the land.

The income stream of an income-producing property can be curtailed post-easement by limitations on the number of apartments permitted, elimination of retail show windows or signs, or use limitations. The loss of the right to display signs can have a substantial impact on the income-earning capacity of a property otherwise suitable in part or in whole for retail, restaurant, or bank use. Easement-donee organizations may require sign and advertising restrictions. Ground-floor users are particularly dependent on signs to attract patronage and would not typically be willing to pay as much rent for space that carried with its use prohibitions or limitations on signs. Furthermore, the property will likely be limited in its potential for adaptation to future fashions. The gross income potential as analyzed by the appraiser should reflect reasonable consideration of any such limitations.

Expenses may be greater under the strictures of an easement. The specified level of maintenance required to satisfy the donee, which can be legally enforced, may be in excess of that which an owner would deem prudent. The maintenance of a deteriorating facade or structure, when contraindicated by economics, is one of the most significant of the typical easement requirements. Elaborate terra cotta ornamentation may be nearly impossible to repair or duplicate. Facades may require hand-cleaning if chemicals or abrasives damage the surface. A stucco facade will require periodic replacement. The judgment of the easement donee as to how and when maintenance should be carried out may not coincide with the judgment of the owner.

Real estate taxes may or may not be reduced, depending on how the assessor views the perpetual aspect of the easement. Utility costs may be increased if energy-saving equipment cannot be installed without violating the facade control provisions. Insurance costs may be affected should insurors become aware of the temptation that arson will present when the easement becomes a burden. Easements which do not require that only a replica or the same type of structure can be rebuilt on the easement-encumbered site if the improvements are destroyed have considerable arson potential.

Other costs that can result from easement donations include the preparation of architectural and other documentation for submission to the donee, the cost and time required to provide for periodic inspections, and the costs and time required to meet with representatives of the donee which can range from a minimal requirement all the way to the extensive expense and time required when alterations develop.

The risk associated with ownership of an easement-encumbered property are greater than the risks associated with otherwise equivalent property. Flexibility of response to economic change has been virtually eliminated. Any capitalization rate used to process income from an encumbered property should reflect the heightened risk, to the degree the market recognizes it. The resulting income capitalization will be lower than in the before-easement case.

Recognition of the effects of preservation easements will likely grow; some states require assessors to reflect the effects of preservation easements in their assessments. Lenders have expressed concern that the security for their loans is jeopardized by preservation easements. If the easement follows the mortgage, the issues of release, prepayment, and balance calls arise.

The Sales Data Approach

The sales data approach derives market value through comparison with market transactions involving similar properties. The application of this direct comparison approach in the before-easement valuation becomes crucial for older properties, for which both income and cost approaches are less reliable. What buyers are paying for similar properties not subject to easements is the simple, direct approach to unencumbered market value. Comparison analysis should be applied to the property as a whole and separately to the land. Sale prices in the two categories tend to overlap in older neighborhoods; the distinction as to what improvements contribute to total value is less than clear-cut. If new construction dominates, many of the improved sales will indicate only land value. On the other hand, if renovation or maintenance dominates, most market transactions will include an increment for the improvements. If the improvements have already been renovated, they will probably contribute substantially to market value. This sorting out of the land and improvement components must be accurate in the before-easement valuation, for distortions will be magnified in the after-easement valuation.

The development potential of the property should be fully reflected in the before-easement value, but only as it can be logically and reasonably supported in the market. If the property is in a landmark district where demolition is effectively prohibited, the property should not be valued on the basis of a highest and best use that requires demolition. On the other hand, landmark district controls are not necessarily permanent and in some cases are not enforced. A major loss is the loss of the right to request permission to make alterations or to demolish.

The sales data approach in after-easement valuations will be less relevant until transactions involving easement-encumbered properties can be accumulated, but even one or two can be indicative, provided the buyers were aware of the effects of the easement.

A sales comparison or market approach to the value of the property after imposition of the easement should consider the restrictions imposed on the subject property relative to those of the comparables. If encumbered properties are not available for direct comparison, adjustments can be made to the value before the easement to reflect decreased marketability. For instance, if there is a demonstrable penalty accruing to buildings that are more expensive to maintain, the same type of penalty is appropriate for properties that have become more expensive to maintain by reason of an easement requirement. If subdivision or a higher density is prohibited, sales or properties otherwise similar but with the density potential of the easement-encumbered subject property can constitute the comparables. The costs of making changes required by an easement can cause a further diminution in market value. These costs can be established by comparison or by the actual cost if changes have already been made.

Pitfalls of Easement Valuation

The easement that is donated before renovation generally has a greater potential for value loss than does the easement donated once renovation is underway or complete. Commencement of renovation before an easement is donated is a clear indication that the property owner believes retention of the improvements is more economic than demolition. However, it is reasonable that an owner would plan the donation of a preservation easement and a renovation concurrently, one as the consequence of the other.

Unfortunately, one not uncommon valuation of easements calculates the value of potential new development through income analysis and subtracts from it the value of property improved by the existing building. This is a serious misinterpretation of the before-and-after approach.[2]

Appraisers should be aware of the penalties for overvaluation of preservation easements. These take the form of an extra tax, ranging from a low of 10 percent of the additional tax owed (which also must be paid) resulting from a valuation that is from 150 percent to 200 percent of the correct valuation, to a high of 30 percent of the additional tax owed when the overvaluation exceeds 250 percent of the correct valuation. There are no penalties for taxpayers who have underpaid by less than $1,000 or who have held the subject property for more than five years, but the additional taxes must be paid. The regulations permit a waiver of the penalty "on a showing by the taxpayer that there was a reasonable basis for the valuation or adjusted basis claimed on the return and that the claim was made in good faith." Appraisers who fail to provide properly supported appraisals risk being sued by their clients for recovery of penalties and other damages. The development of appraisal standards in this area will help to preclude such problems.

[2]See Richard J. Roddewig and Jared Shlaes, "Appraising the Best Tax Shelter in History," *The Appraisal Journal,* January, 1982, p. 25.

Bibliography

Books

Andrews, W. *Architecture, Ambition, and Americans*. Revised edition, 1978. New York: Free Press, 1947.

Condit, C.W. *American Building: Materials and Techniques from the Beginning of the Colonial Settlements to the Present*. Chicago: University of Chicago Press, 1964.

———. *The Chicago School of Architecture*. Chicago: University of Chicago Press, 1964.

Dorsey, S.P. *Early English Churches in America 1607-1807*. New York: Oxford University Press, 1952.

Diamonstein, Barbaralee. *Buildings Reborn: New Uses, Old Places*. New York: Harper & Row, 1978.

Fitch, James Marston, Jr. *American Building: The Historical Forces That Shaped It*. New York: Schocken Books, 1973.

Foley, Mary Mix. *The American House*. New York: Harper & Row, 1980.

Harris, Cyril M., editor. *Dictionary of Architecture and Construction*. New York: 1975.

———. *Historic Architecture Sourcebook*. New York: McGraw Hill Book Company, 1977.

Jordy, William H. *American Buildings and Their Architects: The Impact of European Modernism in the Mid-Twentieth Century*. Garden City, New York: Doubleday & Company, 1976.

———. *American Buildings and Their Architects: Progressive and Academic Ideals at the Turn of the Century*. Garden City, New York: Doubleday & Company, 1976.

Pierson, William H., Jr. *American Buildings and Their Architects: The Colonial and Neo-Classical Styles*. Garden City, New York: Anchor Books, Anchor Press/Doubleday, 1976.

———. *American Buildings and Their Architects: The Corporate and Early Gothic Styles*. Garden City, New York: Doubleday & Company, 1978.

Whiffen, Marcus and Koeper, Frederick. *American Architecture, 1607-1976*. Cambridge, Massachusetts: The MIT Press, 1981.

Wolfe, Tom. *From Bauhaus to Our House*. New York: Farrar Straus Giroux, 1981.

Wrenn, Tony P. and Malloy, Elizabeth D. *America's Forgotten Architecture*. New York: Pantheon Books, 1976.

Urban Land Institute. *Adaptive Use: Development Economics, Process and Profiles*. Washington, D.C.: The Urban Land Institute, 1978.

Periodicals

Coughlin, Thomas A., III. "Preservation Easements: Statutory and Tax Planning Issues." *The Preservation Law Reporter*, 2011 National Trust for Historic Preservation, Washington, D.C., 1982.

Dolman, John P. "Incremental Elements of Market Value Due to Historical Significance." *The Appraisal Journal,* July, 1980.

Gordon, Roy L. "Valuing Historically Significant Properties." *The Appraisal Journal,* April, 1974.

Oldham, Sally G. "Historic Properties: Variable Valuations. *The Appraisal Journal,* July 1982.

Oldham, Sally G. and Jandl, H. Ward. "Preservation Tax Incentives: New Investment Opportunities Under the Economic Recovery Tax Act." *Urban Land,* March 1982.

Reynolds, Anthony and Waldron, William D. "Historical Significance—How Much Is It Worth?" *The Appraisal Journal,* July 1969.

Reynolds, Judith. "Preservation Easements." *The Appraisal Journal,* July 1976.

Shlaes, Jared and Roddewig, Richard J. "Appraising the Best Tax Shelter in History." *The Appraisal Journal,* January 1982.

Technical Bulletins

Easements and Other Legal Techniques to Protect Houses in Private Ownership. Thomas A. Coughlin, III. Historic House Association of America, 1600 H St., N.W., Washington, D.C. 20006.

Preservation Easements. Maryland Historical Trust, 21 State Circle, Anapolis, MD 21401.

General Explanation of the Economic Recovery Tax Act of 1981. Prepared by the staff of the Joint Committee on Taxation, December 29, 1981. U.S. Government Printing Office, Washington, D.C. 1981.

Summary of Preservation Tax Incentives in the Economic Recovery Tax Act of 1981, Information Sheet Number 30. The National Trust for Historic Preservation, Washington, D.C. 1981.

How to Qualify Historic Properties Under the New Law Affecting Easements. Emma Jane Saxe, How to #6. National Park Service, U.S. Department of the Interior, 444 G St., N.W., Washington, D.C. 20240.

Factors Affecting Valuation of Historic Properties. Anthony Reynolds and Judith Reynolds. The National Trust for Historic Preservation, Washington, D.C. 1976.

Review of Rehabilitation Work, Under Section 212 of the Economic Recovery Act of 1981. Technical Preservation Services Division, National Park Service, U.S. Department of the Interior, Washington, D.C. 20240.

Appendix A

The following list is the result of a poll conducted by the *AIA Journal* in 1976. One hundred and fifty architects, historians, and critics were asked to choose the "proudest achievements of American architecture" of the past 200 years. Forty-six responding jurors cited 260 buildings in 140 localities in 36 states, Canada, and Japan. The structures are listed by state and city with the name of the project (in boldface) followed by the architect, the date completed, and the number of jurors citing it.

Arizona

Colorado River (Arizona-Nevada boundary). **Hoover Dam.** Bureau of Reclamation; John Lucian Savage, chief engineer. 1936 (1).

Paradise Valley (near Phoenix). **Taliesin West.** Frank Lloyd Wright. 1938 (6).

Prima County. **San Xavier del Bac.** 1797 (1).

California

Anaheim. **Disneyland.** 1955 (1).

Atherton. **Ritter house.** Wurster, Bernardi & Emmons, Inc. 1957 (1).

Berkeley. **First Church of Christ Scientist.** Bernard Maybeck. 1910 (4). **Havens house.** Harwell Hamilton Harris. 1941 (1) **Hearst Hall,** University of California. Bernard Maybeck. 1899 (1). **Hearst Memorial Gymnasium for Women,** University of California. Bernard Maybeck and Julia Morgan. 1925 (1). **Naval Architecture Building,** University of California. John Galen Howard. 1906 (1). **Northgate,** University of California. John Galen Howard. 1906 (1).

Catalina Island. **Wolfe house.** Rudolf M. Schindler. 1928 (1).

La Jolla. **Salk Institute of Biological Studies.** Louis I. Kahn. 1965 (8).

Los Angeles. **Baldwin Hills Village.** Reginald D. Johnson and Wilson, Merrill & Alexander; Clarence S. Stein, consulting architect. 1942 (1). **Bradbury Building.** George H. Wyman. 1893 (1). **Dodge house.** Irving Gill. 1916 (Demolished) (1). **Eames house.** Charles Eames. 1949 (1). **Fellowship house.** Harwell Hamilton Harris. 1935 (1). **Lovell house.** (demonstration health house) Richard Neutra. 1929 (6). **Schindler house.** Rudolf M. Schindler. 1921 (1). **Watts Towers.** Simon Rodia. 1921-54 (1).

Los Gatos. **Foothill College.** Ernest J. Kump and Masten & Hurd. 1962 (1).

Modesto. **Gallo residence.** Wurster, Bernardi & Emmons, Inc. 1969 (1).

Montecito. **Tremaine residence.** Richard J. Neutra. 1949 (1).

Newport Beach. **Lovell beach house.** Rudolph M. Schindler. 1926 (3).

Oakland. **Oakland Museum.** Kevin Roche, John Dinkeloo & Associates. 1969 (1).

Palm Springs. **Kaufmann desert house.** Richard Neutra. 1947 (1).

Palos Verdes. **Wayfarers' Chapel.** Lloyd Wright. 1951 (2).

Pasadena. **Gamble house.** Charles and Henry Greene. 1908 (4). **Hollyhock house.** Frank Lloyd Wright. 1917 (1). **Hurschler house.** Gregory Ain. 1949 (1).

San Francisco. **Colt Tower.** Arthur Brown Jr. 1934 (1). **Ghirardelli Square.** Wurster, Bernardi & Emmons, architects; Lawrence Halprin & Associates, urban design. 1965 (3). **Golden Gate Bridge.** Irving Morrow, consulting architect; Joseph Strauss, chief engineer. 1937 (3). **Hallide Building.** Willis Polk. 1917 (Restoration by Connor/McLaughlin) (4). **Hyatt Regency Hotel.** John C. Portman & Associates. 1972 (2). **Palace Hotel.** Trowbridge & Livingston. 1909 (1). **Palace of Fine Arts.** (Part of Pan Pacific International Exposition). Bernard Maybeck. 1915; rebuilt, Hans Gerson and Welton Becket. 1965 (1). **St. Mary's Cathedral.** Pietro Belluschi, Pier Luigi Nervi & McSweeney, Ryan & Lee. 1971 (1). **Yerba Buena Club.** (For Golden Gate Exposition) William Wurster. 1939 (Demolished) (1).

Santa Barbara. **County Courthouse.** William Mooser Co. 1929 (1).

Colorado

Boulder. **National Center for Atmospheric Research.** I.M. Pei & Partners. 1967 (1). **University of Colorado.** First building, Day & Klauder. 1922 (1).

Colorado Springs. **U.S. Air Force Academy.** Skidmore, Owings & Merrill. 1956-62 (2).

Denver. **Brown Palace Hotel.** Frank E. Edbrooke & Co. 1892; additions, W.B. Tabler Associates. 1959 (1). **Johns-Manville Headquarters Building.** The Architects Collaborative. 1976 (1).

Morrison. **Red Rock Amphitheater.** Burnham Hoyt. 1941 (1).

Connecticut

New Canaan. **Breuer house I.** Marcel Breuer. 1947 (1). **Johnson residence.** (The "glass house"). Philip Johnson. 1949 (10).

New Haven. **Beinecke Rare Book and Manuscript Library,** Yale University. Skidmore, Owings & Merrill. 1963 (1). **Ingalls Ice Rink,** Yale University. Eero Saarinen & Associates. 1958 (1). **Kline Tower,** Yale University. Philip Johnson & Richard Foster. 1964 (1). **Yale University Art Gallery and Design Center.** (extension of Gallery of Fine Arts opened in 1928) Egerton Swartwout; Louis I. Kahn in association with Douglass Orr. 1953 (2). **Yale University's School of Arts and Architecture Building.** Paul Rudolph. 1963 (4).

District of Columbia

Washington, D.C. **Hirshhorn Museum and Sculpture Garden.** Skidmore, Owings & Merrill. 1974 (1). **Jefferson Memorial.** John Russell Pope; sculptor, Rudolph Evans, 1943 (1). **Lincoln Memorial.** Henry Bacon, architect; Daniel Chester French, sculptor. 1922 (6). **National Gallery of Art.** John Russell Pope. 1941 (1). **National Gallery of Art extension.** I.M. Pei & Partners. Under Construction (1). **Old Executive Office Building.** A.B. Mullett. 1888 (1). **Smithsonian Institution.** (The "Castle") James Renwick. 1849 (1). **U.S. Capitol.** William Thornton, 1793-1802; Benjamin Henry Latrobe, 1803-17; Charles Bulfinch, 1819-29; Robert Mills, 1836-51; Thomas Ustick Walter, 1851-65; West Terrace, Frederick L. Olmstead Sr., 1875 (6). **City of Washington, D.C., L'Enfant plan.** Pierre L'Enfant. 1792 (6). **Washington Monument.** Robert Mills, 1885; original design greatly revised. (4). **White House.** James Hoban, Benjamin Latrobe and others. Begun in 1792 (1).

94

Florida

Cape Kennedy. **Vehicle Assembly Building, Kennedy Space Center.** Max Urbahn & Associates, architects; Roberts & Schaefer Co., engineers. 1966 (2).
  Disney World. **Contemporary Hotel.** Welton Becket & Associates. 1970 (1).
  Sarasota. **Healy guest house.** (The "cocoon house"). Twitchell & Rudolph. 1949 (1).

Georgia

Atlanta. **Hyatt Regency Hotel.** John C. Portman & Associates. 1967 (1).
  Savannah. **Early plan.** James Oglethorpe. c. 1735 (8).

Illinois

Chicago. **Auditorium Building.** (Now Roosevelt University). Adler & Sullivan, 1889; restoration, Harry Weese & Associates; Cromble Taylor, consulting architect. 1967 (3). **Brunswick Building.** Skidmore, Owings & Merrill. 1964 (1). **Carson Pirie Scott & Co.** (Formerly Schleslinger-Mayer Department Store). Louis H. Sullivan. 1899, 1904; Daniel H. Burnham & Co., 1906; Holabird & Root, 1960 (16). Civic Center. C.F. Murphy Associates; Loebl, Schlossman & Bennett and Skidmore, Owings & Merrill. 1965 (1). **Coonley house.** Frank Lloyd Wright. 1908 (1). **Crystal house.** ("The House of Tomorrow," Century of Progress Exposition). George Fred Keck. 1933 (1). **Federal Government Center.** Ludwig Mies van der Rohe; Schmidt, Garden & Erikson; C.F. Murphy Associates; A. Epstein & Sons. 1964 (1). **Home Life Insurance Building.** William La Baron Jenney. 1883 (Demolished) (1). **Illinois Institute of Technology.** Ludwig Mies van der Rohe and Ludwig Hilberseimer; Friedman, Alschuler & Sincere; Holabird & Root; Pace Associates, 1949-52; Skidmore, Owings & Merrill, 1963. (6). **Inland Steel Building.** Skidmore, Owings & Merrill. 1957 (1). **John Hancock Center.** Skidmore, Owings & Merrill. 1969 (6). **Lake Point Tower.** Schipporeit-Heinrich Associates; Graham, Anderson, Probst & White. 1968 (1). **Lake Shore Drive,** 860-880 Lake Shore Drive. Ludwig Mies van der Rohe; Pace Associates; Holsman, Holsman, Klekamp & Taylor. (1951) (5). **Marina City.** Bertrand Goldberg Associates. 1964, 1967 (1). **Marshall Field Wholesale Warehouse.** Henry Hobson Richardson. 1887 (Demolished) (6). **Monadnock Building.** Burnham & Root; Holabird & Roche. 1891, 1893 (9). **Reliance Building.** (Now the 32 North State Building). Daniel H. Burnham & Co. 1895 (8). **Robie house.** (Now Adlai Stevenson Institute of International Affairs). Frank Lloyd Wright. 1909; restoration Frank Lloyd Wright Office and Skidmore, Owings & Merrill, 1967 (11). **Rookery.** Burnham & Root, 1886; remodeled ground story, Frank Lloyd Wright, 1905 (2). **Sears Tower.** Skidmore, Owings & Merrill. 1974 (3) **Studebaker Building.** (Now Fine Arts Building) S.S. Berman. 1884 (1). **Tribune Tower.** Hood & Howells. 1925 (1). **Unity Temple.** (Unitarian Universalist Church and Parish House). Frank Lloyd Wright. 1906 (7). **University of Illinois,** Chicago Campus. Skidmore, Owings & Merrill; C.F. Murphy Associates; A. Epstein & Sons, Inc. 1965, first units (1). **World's Columbian Exposition.** Burnham & Root; Richard M. Hunt; McKim, Mead & White; George B. Post; Peabody & Stearns; Van Brunt & Howe; Charles B. Atwood; Adler & Sullivan; Henry Ives Cobb; Frederick Law Olmsted Sr.; Transportation Building, by Adler & Sullivan, 1893; now remaining is the Midway Plaisance, once the formal entrance to the exposition. (3)
  Highland Park. **Willitts house.** Frank Lloyd Wright. 1902 (1).
  Moline. **Deere & Co. Administrative Center.** Eero Saarinen & Associates. 1965 (3).

Plano. **Farnsworth house.** Ludwig Mies van der Rohe. 1950 (5).

Winnetka. **Crow Island School.** Eliel and Eero Saarinen; Perkins, Wheeler & Will. 1940 (1).

Indiana

Columbus. **Tabernacle Church of Christ.** Eliel Saarinen. 1942 (1).

Iowa

Des Moines. **American Republic Insurance Co.** Skidmore, Owings & Merrill. 1965 (1).

Kentucky

Frankfort. **State House.** Gideon Shryock. 1833 (1).

Lexington. **Transylvania College.** Gideon Shryock. 1833 (1).

Lousiana

New Orleans. **Madame John's Legacy.** c. 1728 (1). **Superdome.** Curtis & Davis. 1975 (1). **Vieux Carre.** Sieur Jean Baptiste Lemoyne de Bienville, founder. 1718 (2).

Vacherie. **Oak Alley.** George Swaney, 1830; restored, Koch & Wilson, 1925 (1).

Maryland

Annapolis. **Annapolis, early plan.** Sir Francis Nicholson. 1695 (1). **U.S. Naval Academy.** 1845- (1).

Columbia. **New City of Columbia.** The Rouse Co., Morton Hoppenfeld, chief planner. 1962- (1).

Massachusetts

Berkshire County. **Hancock Shaker Village.** 1790-1960 (2).

Boston. **Boston Back Bay.** Original plan by Arthur Gilman, accepted in 1856 (2). **Boston park system.** (Often called the city's "emerald necklace"). Frederick Law Olmsted Sr. 1879 (3). **Boston New City Hall.** Kallman, McKinnel & Knowles, Campbell Aldrich & Nulty, Le Messurier & Associates. 1968 (12). **Boston Old City Hall.** Gridley J. Fox Bryand and Arthur Gilman, 1865; restoration, Anderson Notter Associates Inc. (1). **Boston Public Library.** McKim, Mead & White, 1887; addition, Philip Johnson, 1971 (4). **Boston State House.** Charles Bulfinch, 1798; rear extension, Charles E. Bringham, 1895; wings, R. Clipson Sturgis, 1916 (2). **Christian Science Church Center.** I.M. Pei & Partners. 1971 (2). **Faneuil Hall.** John Smibert, 1740-42; Charles Bulfinch, 1805-06; restoration of market area, the Rouse Co., and Benjamin Thompson & Associates, 1975 (1). **John Hancock Tower.** I.M. Pei & Partners. 1975 (2). **Louisburg Square.** Plan by S.P. Fuller, 1826; constructed, 1834-47 (1). **Old West Church.** Asher Benjamin. 1806 (1). **Quincy Market complex.** Alexander Parris. 1824-26 (1). **Tremont House.** Isaiah Rogers. 1826 (Demolished) (1). **Trinity Church,** Boston. Henry Hobson Richardson. 1877 (12).

Cambridge. **Carpenter Center for the Visual Arts,** Harvard University. Le Corbusier, with

Serf, Jackson & Gourley. 1963 (1). **Harvard Graduate Center.** The Architects Collaborative 1950 (1). **Holyoke Center,** Harvard University. Serf, Jackson & Gourley. 1965 (2). **Massachusetts Institute of Technology Chapel.** Eero Saarinen & Associates. 1955 (1). **Peabody Terrace,** Harvard University. (Married students housing). Serf, Jackson & Gourley. 1964 (4). **Sever Hall,** Harvard University. Henry Hobson Richardson. 1880 (1). **Stoughton house.** Henry Hobson Richardson. 1883 (1).

> Dedham. **Fairbanks house.** c. 1636 (1).
>
> Hingham. **Old Ship Meeting House.** c. 1681, widened 1731 and 1755; restored 1930 (2).
>
> Ipswich. **Whipple House.** c. 1640 (1).
>
> Lincoln. **Gropius house.** Walter Gropius. 1938 (2).
>
> North Easton. **Gate lodge,** Ames residence. Henry Hobson Richardson. 1881 (1).
>
> Salem. **Gardiner-White-Pingree house.** Samuel McIntire. 1805 (1).
>
> Topsfield. **Parson Cape house.** 1683 (1).
>
> Quincy. **Crane Memorial Library.** Henry Hobson Richardson. 1883 (4).

Michigan

Bloomfield Hills. **Cranbrook Institutions.** Eliel Saarinen. 1927-43 (4).

> Detroit. **Dodge Half-Ton Truck Factory.** Albert Kahn Associated Architects & Engineers, Inc. 1938 (3). **Freer house.** Wilson Eyre Jr. 1890 (1).
>
> Harbor Springs. **Douglas house.** Richard Meier & Associates. 1975 (1).
>
> Midland. **Dow home.** Alden B. Dow. 1935 (1).
>
> Muskegon. **St. Francis de Sales church.** Marcel Breuer and Herbert Beckhard. 1967 (1).
>
> Warren. **General Motors Technical Center.** Saarinen, Saarinen & Associates; Smith, Hichman & Grylls, Inc. 1956 (3).
>
> Wayne County. **Northland Regional Shopping Center.** Victor Gruen Associates. 1954 (1).
>
> Ypsilanti. **Ford Motor Co., Willow Run Bomber Plant.** Albert Kahn Associated Architects and Engineers, Inc. 1943 (1).

Minnesota

Minneapolis. **Cedar Square West.** Ralph Rapson & Associates. 1973 (1). **Christ Lutheran Church.** Eliel Saarinen. 1949 (1). **IDS Center.** Philip Johnson/John Burgee, in association with Edward F. Baker Associates. 1972 (1).

> Owatonna. **National Farmer's Bank.** Louis Sullivan. 1908 (1).

Missouri

Kansas City. **Liberty Memorial.** Harold Van Burean Magonigle. 1926 (1).

> St. Louis. **Climatron,** Botanical Gardens. Murphy & Mackey; dome, R. Buckminster Fuller. 1960 (1). **Eads Bridge.** James Buchanan Eads. 1874 (2). **Gateway arch.** (Formerly named the Jefferson Westward Expansion Memorial). Eero Saarinen & Associates. 1967 (9). **LaClede Town.** Chloethiel Woodward Smith & Associated Architects. 1966 (1). **Monsanto Cafeteria.** The Kling Partnership. 1967 (1). **Wainwright Building.** Adler & Sullivan, Charles K. Ramsey, 1891; competition for restoration and addition won in 1974 by Hastings & Chivetta and Mitchell/Glurgola Associates. (8).

Nebraska

Lincoln. **Nebraska State Capitol.** Bertram Grosvenor Goodhue. 1932 (3).

New Hampshire

Exeter. **Phillips Exeter Academy Library.** Louis I. Kahn. 1972 (1).

New Jersey

Princeton. **Princeton University, Nassau Hall.** William Shippen & Robert Smith, 1756; restoration, John Notman 1810-65 (1).
  Radburn. **Radburn.** Clarence Stein and Henry Wright. 1829- (7).

New Mexico

Corrales. **Zomehouse.** Steve Baer. 1972 (1).
  Taos. **San Francisco de Taos.** c. 1772 (1).

New York

Albany. **New York State Capitol.** Competition winner, Augustus Laver and Thomas W. Fuller; architects, Leopold Eidlitz and Henry Hobson Richardson. 1881 (1).
  Buffalo. **Larkin Building.** Frank Lloyd Wright. 1905 (Demolished) (5). **Martin house.** Frank Lloyd Wright. 1904 (1). **Prudential (Guaranty) Building.** Louis Sullivan. 1895 (4).
  New York. **Brooklyn Bridge.** John A. and Washington Roebling, engineers. 1883 (11). **CBS Building.** Eero Saarinen & Associates. 1965 (2). **Central Park.** Frederick Law Olmsted Sr. and Calvert Vaux. 1859-76 (7). **Chrysler Building.** William Van Alen. 1930 (1). **City Hall.** Mangin & McComb, 1811; interiors restored under Grosvenor Atterbury, 1902-20, and exteriors under Shreve, Lamb & Harmon, 1959. (1). **Dakota Apartments.** Henry J. Hardenbergh. 1884 (1). **Empire State Building.** Shreve, Lamb & Harmon. 1931 (2). **Flatiron building.** Daniel H. Burnham & Co. 1902 (2). **Ford Foundation Building.** Kevin Roche, John Dinkeloo Associates, 1967 (11). **Grand Central Terminal.** Reed & Stern and Warren & Wetmore. 1903-13 (10). **Haughwout Building.** J.P. Gaynor. 1857 (2). **Lever house.** Skidmore, Owings & Merrill. 1952 (11). **Manufacturers Hanover Trust Co.** Skidmore, Owings & Merrill. 1954 (1). **McGraw-Hill Building.** Raymond M. Hood, with Godley & Fouilhoux. 1931 (1). **New York Public Library.** Carrere & Hastings. 1901 (1). **Pennsylvania Station.** McKim, Mead & White. 1910 (Demolished) (4). **Rockefeller Center.** Initial project: Reinhard & Hofmeister; Corbett, Harrison & MacMurray; Hood & Fouilhoux. 1940 (22). **St. Patrick's Cathedral.** James Renwick. 1858-79 (1). **Seagram Building.** Mies van der Rohe and Philip Johnson; Kahn & Jacobs. 1958 (15). **Solomon R. Guggenheim Museum.** Frank Lloyd Wright. 1959 (6). **Statue of Liberty.** Frederic Bartholdi, sculptor; Gustave Eiffel, engineer; Richard Morris Hunt, architect of the base. 1886 (1). **Temple Emanu-El.** Leopold Eidlitz. 1868 (Demolished) (1). **Trans World Airlines Terminal,** Kennedy Airport. Eero Saarinen & Associates. 1961 (3). **Trinity church,** New York City. Richard Upjohn, 1846; bronze doors by Richard M. Hunt. (1). **United Nations Secretariat Building.** International Committee of Architects, Wallace K. Harrison, Chairman. 1947-53 (1). **University Club.** McKim, Mead & White. 1899 (1). **Verrazano-Narrows Bridge.** Ammann & Whitney, engineers; consulting architects: John B. Peterkin, Amar Embury II, Edward D. Stone.

98

1962 (1). **Woolworth Building.** Cass Gilbert. 1913 (1). **World Trade Center.** Minoru Yamasaki & Associates and Emery Roth & Sons; north tower topped out, 1970; south tower, 1971 (1).

Rochester. **First Unitarian Church.** Louis I. Kahn. 1964 (2).

Syracuse. **Everson Museum of Art.** I.M. Pei & Partners; associated architects: Pederson, Hueber, Hares & Glavin, 1968 (1).

West Point. **U.S. Military Academy.** 1778 (1).

North Carolina

New Bern. **Tryon Palace.** (Also called Governor's Palace). John Hawks, 1767; reconstructed, William Graves Perry of Perry, Shaw, Hepburn, 1952-59 (1).

Ohio

Akron. **University of Akron's Edwin J. Thomas Hall of Performing Arts.** Caudill Rowlett Scott; Schaefer, Flynn & Van Dijk. 1973 (1).

Cincinnati. **Cincinnati Union Station.** Fellheimer & Wagner. 1933 (partly demolished) (1). **Springer Music Hall.** Hannaford & Proctor. 1878 (1).

Oklahoma

Bartlesville. **Price Tower.** Frank Lloyd Wright. 1952 (1).

Norman. **Bavinger house.** Bruce Goff. 1955 (2).

Oregon

Portland. **Coliseum.** Skidmore, Owings & Merrill. 1960 (1). **Civic Auditorium Forecourt.** Lawrence Halprin & Associates. 1966 (2). **Watzek house.** John Yeon, designer; A.E. Doyle & Associates, architects. 1937 (1).

Pennsylvania

Bear Run. **Falling Water,** Edgar Kaufmann house. Frank Lloyd Wright. 1937 (17).

Germantown. **Cliveden.** Benjamin Chew, owner. 1748 (1). **Green Tree Tavern.** Daniel Pastorius, owner. 1748 (1). **Wyck.** Haines house, 1690; remodeled in 1824 by William Strickland. (1).

Paoli. **Esherick house and studio.** Wharton Esherick. 1926 (1).

Philadelphia. **Carl Mackley houses.** Kastner & Stonorov, with W. Barney. 1935 (1). **Christ Church.** 1744; steeple, Robert Smith, 1755. (1). **Fairmount Water Works.** Frederick Graff. 1822 (2). **Independence Hall.** Edmond Wooley and Andrew Hamilton, 1756; removal of old wings, Robert Mills, 1811; new spire, William Strickland, 1829; reconstruction, T. Mellon Rogers, 1897; restoration by city under auspices of Philadelphia chapter/AIA, 1912-13; restoration, National Park Service (3). **Pennsylvania Academy of Fine Arts.** Furness & Hewitt, 1876, restored, 1976, Hyman Miller of Day & Zimmerman Associates (6). **Philadelphia City Hall.** John McArthur Jr. and Thomas U. Walter, 1881 (2). **Philadelphia early plan.** Thomas Holme. 1683 (3). **Philadelphia Saving Fund Society Building.** George Howe & William Lescaze. 1932 (15). **Provident Life and Trust Co.** Frank Furness. 1879 (1). **Richards Laboratory for Research in Medicine,** University of Pennsylvania. Louis I. Kahn. 1960 (6). Venturi & Rauch. 1964 (2).

Pittsburgh. **Allegheny County Courthouse and Jail.** Henry Hobson Richardson. 1887 (5). Chatham Village. Ingham & Boyd, architects; Clarence S. Stein and Henry Wright, site planners. 1930 (3).

Rhode Island

Bristol. **Low house.** McKim, Mead & White. 1887 (2).
 Middletown. **Sturtevant house.** Dudley Newton. 1872 (1).
 Newport. **Newport Casino.** McKim, Mead & White. 1881 (1). **Watts Sherman house.** Henry Hobson Richardson. 1876 (1).

South Carolina

Charleston. **St. Michael's Episcopal Church.** Samuel Cardy, probable architect. 1761 (1).

South Dakota

Pennington County. **Mount Rushmore National Memorial.** Sculptor, Gutzon Borglum. 1941 (1).

Tennessee

Tennessee Valley. **Tennessee Valley Authority.** TVA and Bureau of Reclamation; Roland Wank, architect; Arthur Morgan, engineer. 1933- (5).

Texas

Forth Worth. **Kimball Art Museum.** Louis I. Kahn. 1972 (3).
 Houston. **Astrodome.** Wilson, Morris, Crain & Anderson. 1965 (1). **Pennzoil Place.** Philip Johnson and John Burgee; S.I. Morris Associates. 1976 (1). **Rice University.** Original campus. Cram, Goodhue & Ferguson. 1912 (1). **Tenneco Building.** Skidmore, Owings & Merrill. 1963 (1).
 San Angelo. **San Angelo High School.** Caudill Rowlett Scott Inc. 1959 (1).

Virginia

Chantilly. **Dulles International Airport.** Eero Saarinen & Associates; associated architect and consultant, Ellery Husted. 1962 (17).
 Charles City County. **Westover plantation.** c. 1730 (1).
 Charlottesville. **Monticello.** Thomas Jefferson, 1769-70; remodeled by Jefferson, 1796-1809; restoration, Milton I. Grigg, 1936-38 (9). **University of Virginia,** Jeffersonian campus. Thomas Jefferson, aided by William Thornton and Benjamin Latrobe, 1822-26; annex by Robert Mills, 1851; rotunda burned in 1895; rebuilt to design by Stanford White in 1900; restored by Ballou & Justice; consultant, Frederick D. Nichols, 1976 (29).
 Greenway. **Madeira School.** Arthur Cotton Moore Associates. 1976. (1).
 Mount Vernon. **Mount Vernon.** Augustine Washington, original owner, 1743; alterations, 1757-58, 1773-79; numerous and ongoing restorations; major changes in the late 19th and early 20th centuries, with 1799, date of George Washington's death, the restoration focus. (2).

Reston. **The New City of Reston's Lake Anne Center.** Whittlesey, Conklin & Rossant. 1966 (1).

Westmoreland County. **Stratford.** 1730 (3).

Williamsburg. **The City of Williamsburg,** restoration. Architectural development of the plan: Perry, Shaw & Hepburn; Colonial Williamsburg. (5).

Washington

Seattle. **Space Needle.** John Graham & Co. 1962 (1).

Tacoma. **Weyerhauser Headquarters.** Skidmore, Owings & Merrill. 1971 (2).

Wisconsin

Racine. **Johnson Wax Co. Administration Building and Laboratory Tower.** Frank Lloyd Wright. 1939, 1949 (1).

Spring Green. **Taliesin East.** Frank Lloyd Wright. 1911 (3).

Wyoming

Yellowstone National Park. **Old Faithful Inn.** Central portion built in 1903, Robert C. Reamer, architect; wings added in 1913 and 1927. (1).

Canada

Montreal. **U.S. Pavilion, Expo '67.** R. Buckminster Fuller/Fuller & Sadao, Inc.; architects for the exhibition: Cambridge Seven Associates. 1967 (Destroyed) (2).

Japan

Osaka. **U.S. Pavilion, Expo '70.** David, Brody, Chermayeff, Geismar & de Harak. 1970 (1).

General

Geodesic Dome and Dymaxion House. R. Buckminster Fuller. (5).

Appendix B

State Historic Preservation Officers

Chief, History & Archaeology
Department of Natural Resources
619 Warehouse Ave., Rm. 210
Anchorage, AK 99501
206-583-0150, ask for Anchorage
907-274-4676

Chief, Natural & Cultural Resources
Arizona State Parks
1688 West Adams
Phoenix, AZ 85007
602-255-4174

Director, Historical Commission
59 South Prospect St.
Hartford, CT 06106
203-566-3005

Director, Division of Architecture,
    History, Records Management
Department of State, The Capitol
Tallahassee, FL 32304
904-488-3965

Historic Preservation Officer
Land and Natural Resources
P.O. Box 621
Honolulu, HI 96809
FTS: 556-0220, ask for Honolulu
548-6550

Director, Department of Conservation
605 State Office Building
400 S. Spring St.
Springfield, IL 62706
217-782-6302 or 8-956-6302

Director, Alabama Department of
    Archives & History
Archives & History Building
Montgomery, AL 36104
202-832-6622

Historical Preservation Office
Department of Parks & Recreation
P.O. Box 2390
Sacramento, CA 95811
916-445-8006

Director, Department of Housing
    & Community Development
1133 N. Capitol St., N.W.
Washington, D.C. 20001
202-535-1282

Historic Preservation Section
Department of Natural Resources
270 Washington St., S.W.
Atlanta, GA 30334
404-656-2840

Director, Iowa State History
    Department, Historic Preservation
26 E. Market St.
Iowa City, IA 53340
319-353-4186 or 6949

Director, Department of Natural Resources
608 State Office Building
Indianapolis, IN 46204
317-232-4020

Director, Historic Preservation
Suite 500, Continental Building
Markham and Main Sts.
Little Rock, AR 72201
501-371-2763

Historic Preservation Officer
Colorado Heritage Center
1300 Broadway
Denver, CO 80203
303-892-2136 or FTS 839-2136

Director, Division of Historical
& Cultural Affairs
Hall of Records
Dover, DE 19901

Director, Department of Parks
& Recreation
Government of Guam
P.O. Box 682
Agana, GQ 96910
Overseas Operator 477-9620/21, ext. 4

Historic Preservation Coordinator
Idaho Historical Society
610 N. Julia Davis Dr.
Boise, ID 83706
208-384-2120

Executive Director
Kansas State Historical Society
120 W. 10th St.
Topeka, KS 66612
913-296-3251

Executive Director & SHPO
Kentucky Heritage Commission
104 Bridge St.
Frankfort, KY 40601
502-564-6683

Historic Preservation Officer
Maryland Historic Trust
21 State Circle
Annapolis, MD 21401

Director, Minnesota Historical Society
690 Cedar St.
St. Paul, MN 55101
612-296-2747

Director, Montana Historical Society
225 N. Roberts St.
Helena, MT 59601
406-449-2694

Director, Nebraska State Historical Society
1500 R St.
Lincoln, NE 68508
402-471-3270, or FTS 541-3270

Historic Preservation Officer
State Planning Division
505 Don Gaspar Ave.
Santa Fe, NM 87503
505-827-2108

Director, Ohio Historical Society
Interstate 71 at 17th Ave.
Columbus, OH 43211
614-466-3852

Assistant Secretary
Office of Program Development
P.O. Box 44247
Baton Rouge, LA 70804
504-925-3884, or 3880

Director, Historic Preservation Commission
55 Capitol St.
Augusta, ME 04330
207-289-2133

Historic Preservation Officer
Department of Cultural Resources
109 E. Jones St.
Raleigh, NC 27611
919-733-7305

Commissioner, Department of Resources &
Economic Development
P.O. Box 856
Concord, NH 03301
603-271-3483 or 3558

Historic Preservation Officer
Historic Preservation & Archeology
Capitol Complex
Carson City, NV 89701
702-885-5138

Historic Preservation Officer
Oklahoma Historical Society
Historical Building
Oklahoma City, OK 73105
405-521-2491

Executive Director
Massachusetts Historical Commission
294 Washington St.
Boston, MA 02108
617-727-8470

Director, Michigan History Division
Department of State
Lansing, MI 48918
517-373-6362

Director, Mississippi Dept. of
   Archives and History
P.O. Box 571
Jackson, MS 39205
601-254-6218

Superintendent, State Historical Society of
   North Dakota
Liberty Memorial Bulding
Bismarck, ND 58501
701-224-2667

Commissioner, Department of
   Environmental Protection
P.O. Box 1390
Trenton, NJ 08625
609-292-2885

Commissioner, Parks & Recreation
Agency Building #1
Empire State Plaza
Albany, NY 12238
518-474-0468

State Parks Superintendent
525 Trade St., S.E.
Salem, OR 97310
503-378-6305

Historic Preservation Officer
Historic & Museum Commission
P.O. Box 1026
Harrisburg, PA 17120
717-787-2891

Director, State Archives Department
1430 Senate St.
Columbia, SC 29211
803-758-5816

Historic Preservation Officer
Department of Resources & Development
Mariana Islands
Saipan, TQ 96950

Executive Director
Texas Historical Commission
P.O. Box 12276, Capitol Station
Austin, TX 78711
512-475-3092

Planning Director
Virgin Islands Planning Board
Charlotte Amalie
St. Thomas, VI 00801
Commercial 9-809-774-1726

Director, State Historical Society
816 State St.
Madison, WI 53706
608-262-3266

Office of Cultural Affairs
La Fortaleza
San Juan, PR 00905
9-809-724-2100: Institute of P.R.
9-809-724-0700

Historic Preservation Officer
University of South Dakota
Alumni House
Vermillion, SD 57069
605-677-5314

Historic Preservation Officer
Community & Cultural Affairs
Northern Mariana Islands
Saipan, TQ 96950

Historic Preservation Officer
Utah Historical Society
307 W. 200 S., Suite 1000
Salt Lake City, UT 84101
801-533-5755

Secretary, Agency of Development and
    Community Affairs
Pavilion Office Building
Montpelier, VT 05602
802-828-3221

Commissioner, Department of Culture &
    History
State Capitol Complex
Charleston, WV 25304
304-348-0244

Director, Rhode Island Department of
    Community Affairs
150 Washington St.
Providence, RI 02903
401-277-2850

Executive Director
Tennessee Historical Commission
4721 Trousdale Dr.
Nashville, TN 37220
615-741-2371

Historic Preservation Officer
Dept. of Public Works
Government of American Samoa
Pago Pago, TQ 96799

Executive Director
Virginia Historic Landmarks Commission
221 Governor St.
Richmond, VA 23219
804-786-3143

Historic Preservation Officer
111 W. 21st Ave.
KL-11
Olympia, WA 98504
206-753-4011

Mrs. Jan L. Wilson
Historic Preservation Officer
Wyoming Recreation Commission
604 E. 25th St., Box 309
Cheyenne, WY 82001
307-777-7695

Federal Preservation Officers and Agency Liaisons

The representatives with stars (*) preceding
their names are the primary Federal Preservation Officers for their departments or agencies and have the authority to approve National Register nominations.

Department of Agriculture

*Coordinator, Office of Environmental Quality Activities
Department of Agriculture
Room 412-A, Administration Building
Washington, D.C. 20250
202-447-3493

Assistant Director, Dispersed Recreation
Forest Service
Department of Agriculture
Box 2417, Room 4150, South Building
Washington, D.C. 20013
202-447-8618

Director, Social Sciences
Soil Conservation Service, USDA
P.O. Box 2890
Department of Agriculture
Washington, D.C. 20013
202-755-9701

Farmers Home Administration
Room 6302, South Building
Washington, D.C. 20250

Department of Commerce

*Chief, Program and Policy Staff
Office of Administrative Services
Department of Commerce
Room 6414
Washington, D.C. 20230
202-377-3322

Department of Defense

*Director, Real Property and Natural Resources Division
Office of the Assistant Secretary of Defense
(Manpower, Reserve Affairs and Logistics)
Washington, D.C. 20301
202-697-7277

*DAEN-CWP-P
Plan Formulation and Evaluation Branch,
Planning Division
Directorate of Civil Works
Corps of Engineers
Department of the Army
Washington, D.C. 20314
202-272-0131

U.S. Marine Corps
Head, Historical Branch
Reference Section
Headquarters, Marine Corps
Washington Navy Yard, Building 58
Washington, D.C. 20374
202-433-3864

U.S. Marine Corps
Historical Branch
HQ Marine Corps
Washington, D.C. 20380

DAEN-FEB-P
Department of the Army
Washington, D.C. 20314

Special Assistant for the Environment to the
Deputy Assistant Secretary
for Economic Development
Economic Development Administration
Department of Commerce, Room 7019
14th and Constitution Ave., N.W.
Washington, D.C. 20230
202-377-4208

Program Support and Regulatory
Branch Head
Installations Planning Division (Code 202A)
Naval Facilities Engineering Command
200 Stovall St.
Alexandria, VA 22332
202-325-7343

AF-LEEV
The Pentagon, Room 5D471
Washington, D.C. 20330
202-697-2093

Department of Energy

Assistant Secretary for Environment
Department of Energy, EV-l
Room 4G0H5, Forrestal Building
1000 Independence Ave., S.W.
Washington, D.C. 20585

Chief, Registration and Procedures Branch
NEPA Affairs Division, 4G064
U.S Department of Energy
825 N. Capitol St., N.E., Rm. 3000
Washington, D.C. 20426
202-357-8228

Advisor to the Commission
Federal Energy Regulatory Commission
Department of Energy
825 N. Capitol St., N.E., Rm. 3000
Washington, D.C. 20426
202-357-8228

Assistant Director, Installations Planning
   Division
(Code 202A)
Naval Facilities Engineering Command
200 Stovall St.
Alexandria, VA 22332
202-325-0521

Department of Housing and Urban Development

*Assistant Secretary for Community Plan-
   ning and Development, Room 7100
Department of Housing and
   Urban Development
Washington, D.C. 20410
202-755-6270

Director, Office of Environmental Quality
Department of Housing and
   Urban Development
Room 7274
Washington, D.C. 20410
202-755-6300

Historic Preservation Officer
Environmental Management Division
Department of Housing and
   Urban Development
Room 7274
Washington, D.C. 20410
202-755-6300

Department of Health and Human Services

*Deputy Director
Office of Environmental Affairs
Department of Health and Human Services,
   Room 537F
200 Independence Ave., S.W.
Washington, D.C. 20201
202-472-9740

Department of the Interior

Assistant Secretary for Fish and Wildlife
   and Parks
Department of the Interior
Washington, D.C. 20240
Attn: Mr. Ric Davidge

*Division of Recreation
Bureau of Land Management
Department of the Interior
Washington, D.C. 20240
202-343-9353

*Bureau of Land Management
Department of the Interior
Washington, D.C. 20240
202-343-9353

*Division of Property and General Services
Bureau of Mines
Department of the Interior
Washington, D.C. 20240
202-343-4750

108

Assistant Director
Technology and Development
Department of the Interior
Washington, D.C. 20240
202-343-4341

Office of Surface Mining
Department of Interior, South Building
Room 116 South
Washington, D.C. 20240
202-343-2184

*Chief of Environmental Affairs
760, U.S. Geological Survey
National Center, 12201 Sunrise Valley Drive
Reston, VA 22092
202-860-7493

*Assistant Director, Cultural Resources
National Park Service
Department of the Interior, Room 1226
Washington, D.C. 20240
202-343-7625

*Chief, Office of Environmental Affairs
Water and Power Resources Service
Department of the Interior
Washington, D.C. 20240
202-343-4991

*Senior Service Archeologist
MC-203
Water and Power Resources Service
P.O. Box 25007 DFC
Denver, CO 80225
303-234-4348

U.S. Fish and Wildlife Service
Department of the Interior
Washington, D.C. 20245
202-343-5333

*U.S. Fish and Wildlife Service
Department of the Interior
Washington, D.C. 20245
202-272-3365

*Bureau of Indian Affairs
Code 204
1951 Constitution Ave., N.W.
Washington, D.C. 20245
202-343-8248

Department of Justice

*Chief, Policy and Planning Group
Facilities Management Section
Property, Management and Procurement Staff
Justice Management Division, Room 1618
U.S. Department of Justice
10th and Pennsylvania Ave., N.W.
Washington, D.C. 20530
202-633-2175

Department of Transportation

*Office of Environmental Affairs
Room 9422
Department of Transportation
Washington, D.C. 20590
202-426-4298

Commandant (G-FLT/71)
U.S. Coast Guard, 400 7th St., S.W.
Washington, D.C. 20590
202-426-2031
Attn: Lt. Commander Bower

Environmental Specialist
Federal Aviation Administration
AEE-110
800 Independence Ave., S.W., Room 835
Washington, D.C. 20591
202-755-9026

HEV-22
Chief, Environmental Quality Branch
Federal Highway Administration
Department of Transportation
Washington, D.C. 20590
202-426-9173

Director, Office of Program Analysis
Urban Mass Transportation Administration
Department of Transportation
Washington, D.C. 20590
202-426-4020

Department of State

*Assistant Secretary of State
 for Administration
Department of State
Washington, D.C. 20520
202-632-1492

Department of the Treasury

*Assistant Director, Environmental Programs
Room 706
Office of Administrative Programs
Department of the Treasury
Washington, D.C. 20220
202-376-0830

Independent Agencies

*Environmental Protection Specialist
Office of Environmental Review (A-104)
Environmental Protection Agency
Washington, D.C. 20460
202-755-0780

*Room 222
Federal Communications Commission
Washington, D.C. 20554
202-632-6410

Director of Historic Preservation
General Services Administration
Washington, D.C. 20405
202-566-0986

*Chief, Section of Administrative Services
Interstate Commerce Commission
Room 2215, 12th and Constitution Ave.
Washington, D.C. 20243
202-275-7428

*(BXBQ) Facilities Division
NASA Headquarters
Washington, D.C. 20546
202-755-3327

*Chief, Historic Preservation Branch
National Capitol Planning Commission
1325 G St., N.W.
Washington, D.C. 20576
202-724-0205

*N.S.F. Historian
National Science Foundation
Washington, D.C. 20550
202-357-9637

*Small Business Administration
1441 L St., N.W.
Washington, D.C. 20416
202-653-6429

Special Assistant to the Secretary
Smithsonian Institution
Washington, D.C. 20560
202-357-2264

*Office of Natural Resources
Tennessee Valley Authority
Norris, TN 37828
615-632-3338

Program Coordinator
Cultural Resources Program
Division of Land and Forest Resources
Tennessee Valley Authority
Norris, TN 37828
FTS 856-6450

*Office of Construction
Veterans Administration
811 Vermont Ave., N.W.
Washington, D.C. 20420
202-389-3447

110

*International Boundary and
Water Commission
U.S. and Mexico
4110 Rio Bravo
200 IBWC Building
El Paso, TX 79902
915-543-7323

*Senior Staff Member for Historic Preserva-
tion, Urban Affairs, and Land Use
Council on Environmental Quality
722 Jackson Place, N.W.
Washington, D.C. 20006
202-395-5700

Regional Environmental Economist
Regional Impact Analysis Section
Nuclear Regulatory Commission
Washington, D.C. 20555
301-492-8555

*Director, Office of Real Estate
U.S. Postal Service
475 L'Enfant Plaza, S.W.
Washington, D.C. 20260
202-245-5271

Real Estate Specialist
U.S. Postal Service
Office of Real Estate
475 L'Enfant Plaza, S.W.
Washington, D.C. 20260
202-245-5271

National Trust for Historic Preservation Regional Offices

Mid-Atlantic
1600 H St., N.W.
Washington, D.C. 20006
202-673-4203
Ron Lewis, Regional Director
Delaware, District of Columbia, Maryland,
New Jersey, Pennsylvania, Puerto Rico,
Virgin Islands, Virginia, West Virginia.

Midwest
407 S. Dearborn, #710
Chicago, IL 60605
312-353-3419, 3424
Tim Turner, Regional Director
Illinois, Indiana, Iowa, Michigan, Minnesota,
Missouri, North Dakota, Ohio, South Da-
kota, Wisconsin.

Northeast
Old City Hall
45 School St, Second Floor
Boston, MA 02108
617-223-7754
David Gillespie, Regional Director
Connecticut, Maine, Massachusetts, New
Hampshire, New York, Rhode Island, Ver-
mont.

Southern
456 King St.
Charleston, SC 29403
803-724-4711 (FTS: 677-4711)
Dwight Young, Regional Director
Alabama, Arkansas, Florida, Georgia, Kentucky, Louisiana, Mississippi, North Carolina, South Carolina, Tennessee.

Southwest/Plains

210 Colcord Building
Oklahoma City, OK 73102
405-231-5126 (FTS: 736-5126)
Colorado, Kansas, Nebraska, New Mexico, Oklahoma, Texas.

Western

681 Market St., #859
San Francisco, CA 94105
415-974-8420 (FTS: 454-8420)
Hisashi Bill Sugaya, Director
Alaska, Arizona, California, Hawaii, Idaho, Montana, Nevada, Oregon, Utah, Washington, Wyoming, Guam, Micronesia.

NPS Regional Offices

Mid-Atlantic

143 S. Third St.
Philadelphia, PA 19106
215-597-7013
States Administered for Tax Certification Purposes: Connecticut, Maine, Massachusetts, New Hampshire, New Jersey, New York, Rhode Island, Vermont, Delaware, Maryland, Pennsylvania, Virginia, West Virginia, District of Columbia.

The address for the historic preservation program which administers the Department of the Interior's preservation tax incentive program is: Historic Preservation Tax Incentives, Archeology and Historic Preservation, National Park Service, Washington, D.C., 20240.

Addresses for the NPS Regional Offices which review certification applications are as follows:

Southeast

75 Spring St., N.W.
Atlanta, GA 30303
404-221-5185
States Administered for Tax Certification Purposes: Alabama, Florida, Georgia, Kentucky, Mississippi, North Carolina, South Carolina, Tennessee, Puerto Rico, Virgin Islands.

Southwest

Old Santa Fe Trail
P.O. Box 728
Santa Fe, NM 87501
505-988-6388
Albuquerque: 505-474-5944
States Administered for Tax Certification Purposes: Louisiana, Arkansas, Oklahoma, New Mexico, Texas.

Index